Etchings 34.1

Literary and Fine Arts Magazine of the
University of Indianapolis
Fall 2021

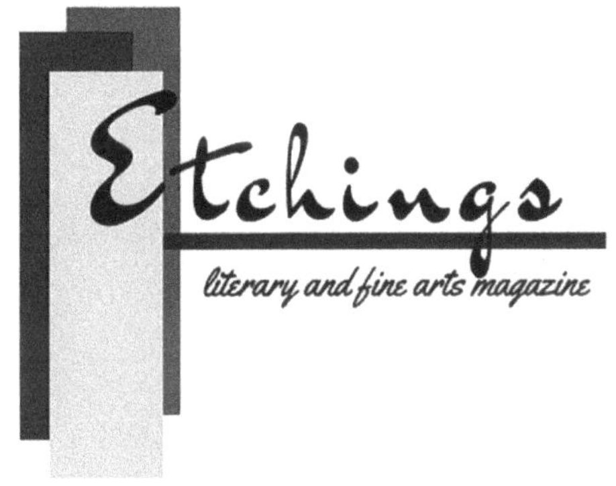

1400 E. Hanna Ave.
Indianapolis, IN 46227

Cover Design by Etchings Staff
Cover Art by Sydney Smith
Printed by IngramSpark
ingramspark.com

Etchings Editorial Staff

Submissions Editor

Danielle Shaw

Managing Editor

Emma Knaack

Design Editors

Olivia Cameron
Ali Viewegh

Staff Editors

Sam Jackson
Kim Owen

Faculty Advisor

Liz Whiteacre

Table of Contents

Announcements

Poetry

Prose

Visual Arts

Audio

***CW is the abbreviation for Content Warning. Please read, view, and listen to these pieces with caution.**

Letter from the Staff

Dear Readers,

Greyhounds have unique experiences, perspectives, and voices. Everyone responds to life and its circumstances and struggles in totally different ways. As readers, we need to respect them no matter where we are in our own stories. This term, we've learned that responses to creative work are subjective and that it is extremely difficult to judge others' pieces and have conversations about them when we can be very emotionally attached to them. We appreciate all of the submissions we received and the opportunity to create this issue.

When creating an issue of *Etchings*, weeks of deep deliberation, disagreements, and compromising take place. We tried our best to judge fairly and encourage diversity in the stories being told. Extreme care and consideration went into selecting and organizing pieces in the magazine. This issue holds precious thoughts, opinions, feelings, and aspects of people's lives. Some of the content in this issue may disturb you, and we've included content warnings for pieces because we want our magazine to be inclusive and safe. There are people who have been silenced for too long on issues that pieces in this issue explore, like rape and sexual assault. We feel some people may have experienced the same thing but haven't reached out and have suffered all by themselves. They need to know there are other survivors and there are those who want to help. It is not helpful to pretend that bad things don't happen or make traumatizing experiences too taboo to speak about. The world isn't very nice, but it could be nicer if we listened to each other. Voices like those with the content warnings should not be silenced as they often highlight parts of society that are avoided or ignored. Sharing can make people feel like they're not alone in their struggles and help us have conversations that spark change.

At the end of this issue, we are including resources for you to learn more about the topics pieces explore and to, perhaps, seek help. We hope you leave this issue with new perspectives, an understanding that it's okay to talk about things that hurt us, and a new appreciation of how talented and brave our Greyhound writers, composers, and artists are. We hope you have a sense of excitement and happiness from reading the non-triggering pieces and that you feel heard and seen by the pieces in the magazine. You can visit our website, etchings.uindy.edu, to read writer statements and learn more about all the pieces from their creators. *Etchings* is a safe space, and we're committed to doing what's right. Reach out to us at etchings@uindy.edu, if you'd like to share your experiences reading this issue.

Respectfully,

The Etchings Team

Fall 2021 Dorlis Gott Armentrout Winners

Judged by Barbara Shoup

First Prize: "Heart Shaped Bruises" by Cassi Dillon (pg 84)

"Heart Shaped Bruises" has a strong voice that speaks a painful truth with simple yet effective language, making the reader feel the speaker's pain through its excellent use of detail. I found the way the last stanza moves toward a single word at the end very moving, as if the poem's speaker is diminishing.

Runner Up: "What Boyfriends Do" by Brandon Hickey (pg 71)

I like how "What Boyfriends Do" puts a spin on a traditional "problems of love" story by making a young gay man the one who feels uncomfortable in a sexual relationship. The story is well written, keeping the reader grounded in time and place, creating tension, and showing that life is more complicated than it may seem.

Fall 2021 Dorlis Gott Armentrout Judge

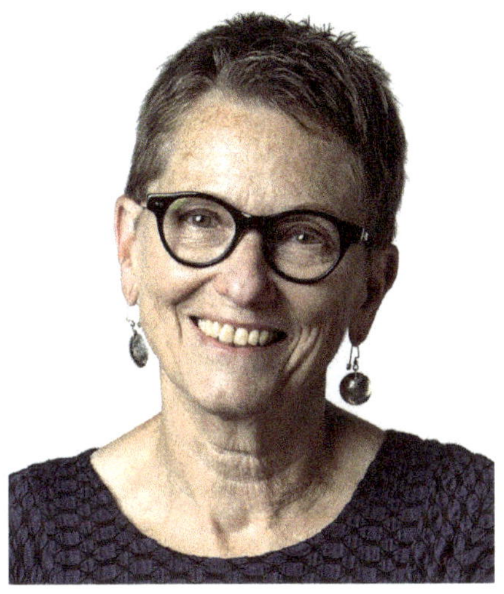

Barbara Shoup is the author of eight novels for adults and young adults, most recently *An American Tune, Looking for Jack Kerouac*, and a memoir, *A Commotion in Your Heart*. She is the co-author of *Novel Ideas: Contemporary Authors Share the Creative Process and Story Matters*. Her short fiction, poetry, essays and interviews have appeared in numerous small magazines, as well as in *The Writer* and *The New York Times* travel section. Currently, she is the Writer-in-Residence at the Indiana Writers Center and a creative writing faculty member of Art Workshop in Assisi.

For a deeper look into Barbara Shoup's work, visit her website:
www.barbarashoup.com

Barbara Shoup Interview

ETCHINGS: What would you say to budding writers struggling to finish and revise a longer piece of work?

BARBARA SHOUP: Be patient. Writing a long piece takes a long time if you do it right—sometimes years—and revising is extremely challenging because there are so many things (and questions) to consider. You need to switch to the analytical part of your head to answer these questions—which doesn't feel creative at all. Yet it is an important part of the creative process. I find it useless to try to revise by going through the manuscript, correcting as I go. Eventually, I start skimming, missing things, and when I get to the end, I know only vaguely what I need to do. So, I use a spreadsheet to track characters, threads, and whatever else I think I need to track for any given novel. When I'm "finished," I have a list of very specific revisions to make. Then I make them, checking them off as I go. Finished is in quotes because I almost always go through this process numerous times before I think a book is ready to send out. Then, when it's bought, the editor will have her own ideas about what the book needs, so I go through it again. This sounds awful, I know. But I actually love revising. Getting the first draft down is the hardest part of writing to me.

E: How do you work through moments of discouragement?

BS: I talk to other writers, blow off steam in my journal, do yoga, take my dog for a walk. I remind myself the moment will pass. I. Keep. On. Writing.

E: Through your work with the Indiana Writers Center, you have supported many emerging writers. What advice do you have for Greyhounds interested in revising their work to prepare for the world of publishing?

BS: Never, ever send a piece out as soon as you've finished it no matter how good you think it may be. An editor only gets one first look at a manuscript and even if she's willing to reconsider the piece with revisions, the ghost of what she read first will always get in the way. So let it sit a while. Stuff that needs to be revised will jump out at you when you take a second look. Take a second pass, but it probably still won't be finished because you can't know what the words on the page are doing because you can't read them without bringing what's in your head to the page. This means you need good critics to help you see the difference between what's actually there. So, lose your ego! Toughen up! Give the piece to readers you know will tell you the truth (probably not your mom or best friend) and ask them to look for what doesn't make sense, what's missing, what doesn't belong, where there's not enough, where there's too much, where you're telling instead of showing. (Of course, it's also good to ask them to tell you what works—and why.) Writing is revising. Self-discipline is a kind of talent. I've interviewed dozens of writers over the years and have found that the better they are, the more likely they are to revise (and revise and revise). Make sure your piece of writing is as good as it possibly can be before you seek publication.

E: In your experience, what has been the most effective way to market your work?

BS: Honestly, I'm horrible at marketing. I always think I'm going to get better at it but I don't, even though I know I owe it to my work. I'd always rather be writing. Writers who are good at marketing send a piece back out the day it's rejected—and keep the cycle going until someone says yes. Writers with books coming out begin preparing for publication months—even a year—before the pub date, setting up interviews, posting on social media. One thing I am good at is posting about/promoting books by writers I know and admire. Cathy Day calls this being a good literary citizen, a term I like. I do it because I really want people to know about those books, but it often turns out that those writers will post something nice about mine. In that way, it's a good marketing tool.

E: From teaching creative writing to working at the Indiana Writers Center, how have you seen your work evolve over the years? What has been a major influence in your writing?

BS: Teaching creative writing for twenty years at Broad Ripple High School Center for the Humanities and the Performing Art taught me pretty much everything I know about writing because I had to figure out what to say to my student writers about their work. Same with every other kind of teaching I've done. There's often a moment, a struggle to explain something, that a light bulb goes on in my head and I say something I didn't know I knew. I love when that happens! Teaching has also been an influence in my work, especially the young adult novels. Bits and pieces of my students and their lives often turn up one way or another in them. But the major influence in my writing is my own life—looking "sideways" at it by way of fiction, trying to understand all that happened and why, and how (for better or worse) it made me who I am.

Anna Elizabeth Gott Memorial Art Awards

The recipients of the UIndy Anna Elizabeth Gott Memorial Art Award were Brittany Beaver and Ezekiel (Zeke) Fredrickson. This award, honoring outstanding senior art and design majors, was endowed as a memorial in 1978 by Anna's sister, Mary E. Gott. Anna Elizabeth Gott had traveled widely in her career with the federal government and, in doing so, developed a deep interest in the great masterpieces of world art. This contest was judged by Art & Design faculty.

Mary E. Gott Awards for Excellence in Art

The recipients of the UIndy Mary E. Gott Award for Excellence in Art were Rebekah Letcher and Hollie Duncan. This award, honoring outstanding junior art and design majors, was endowed in 1984 by UIndy Professor Emeritus Robert Brooker and his wife, Ruth, as a tribute to Mrs. Brooker's aunt, Mary E. Gott. Mary, like her sister Anna, held a government post in Washington, D.C. and loved art. This contest was judged by Art & Design faculty.

2021 Lucy Monro Brooker Poetry Award

There's an accusation about to spill from your lips...

by Hope Coleman

the words already leaking out
and staining the place on the carpet
that your feet have worn bare.

There's an accusation about to spill from your lips...

the words teetering in their final moments,
hesitation evident in the way you
stutter,
falter,
fail
to carry through with the venom
you had intended to spit.
Left now with some weakened,
watered down version
of the words you needed
so desperately,
to say.

There's an accusation about to spill from your lips...

the words holding power,
too much power,
over the fate of this thing the two of you have built.
Too easily could you kill it,
wrapping your words in a vice-like grip,
strangling,
constricting,
spilling
the spark that sustained the two of you
out into the open air.

There's an accusation about to spill from your lips...

the fateful last moments where you can decide
to destroy,
to sustain,
to change
how things are forever. You steel yourself against the fallout,
dig your feet into the carpet, worn bare,
and let the words
spill.

Illustrations for Award

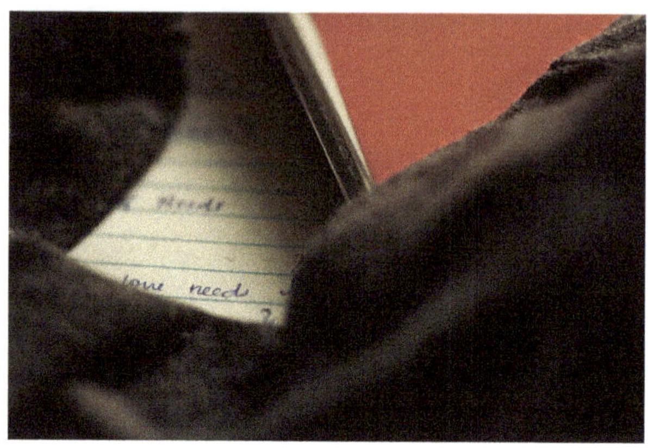

Needs,
Adam Fernandes

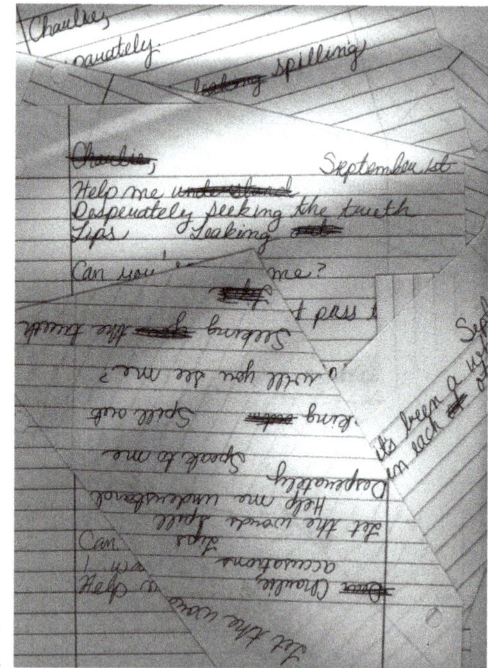

Dear Charlie,
Kristen Taylor

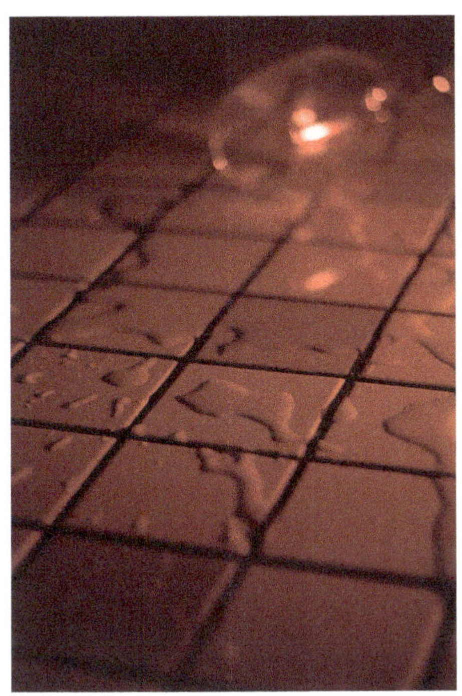

Splatter,
Audrey Kline

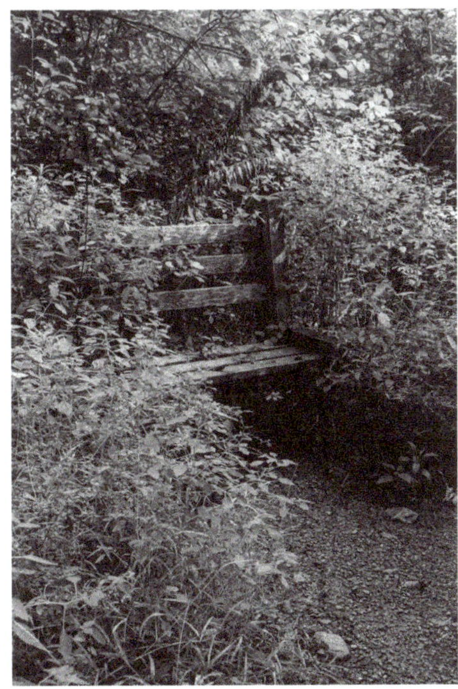

How Long Can Dust Wait,
Jes Brockman Artemiev

Into the Open Air, Jes Brockman Artemiev

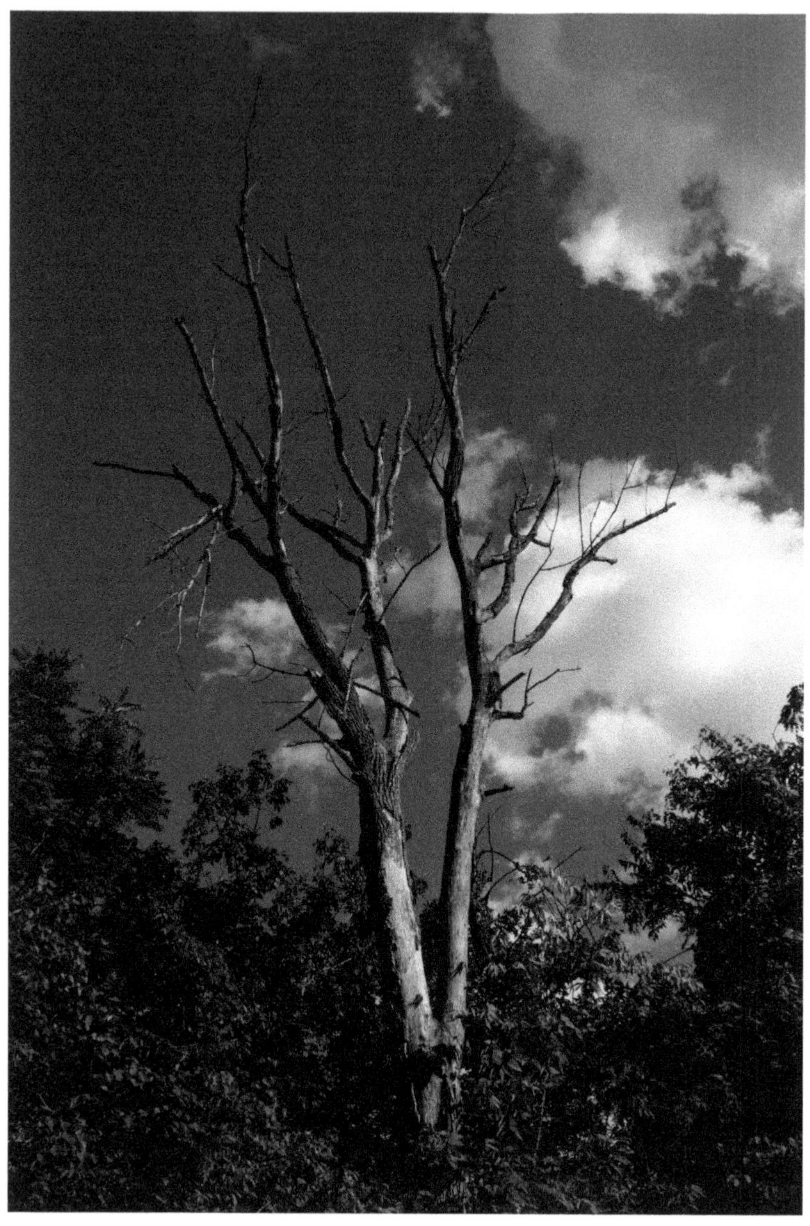

2021 Annual Student Exhibition: Winner in Studio Art

Demeter's Cup

by Emma Warner

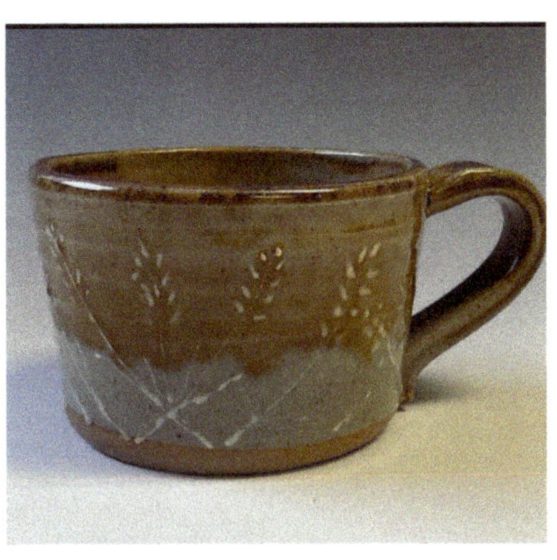

2021 Annual Student Exhibition: Winner in Visual Communication

Instructional Design

by Hannah Jones

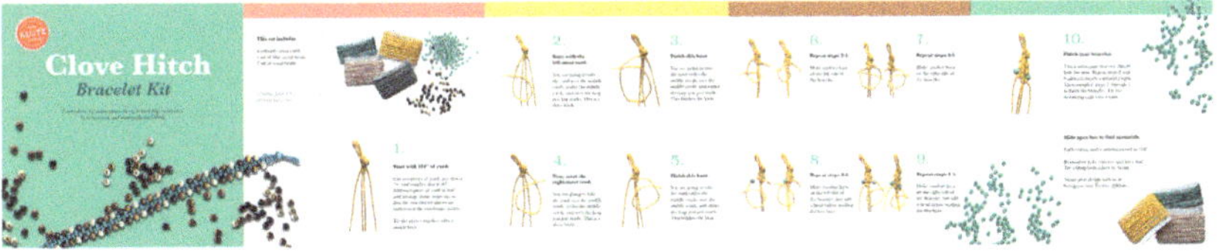

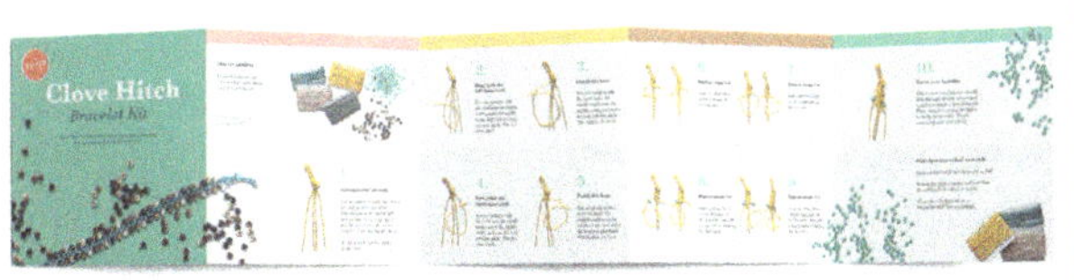

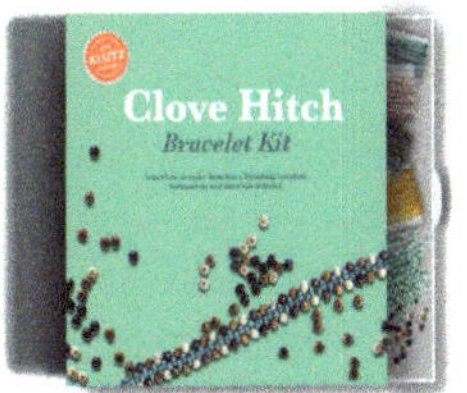

2021 Roberta Lee Brooker Fiction Writing Prize

The Final Notice

by Savannah Harris

At the community play last year, we saw someone beat a horse to death. We were understandably shaken up after the incident; or perhaps it was the true murder—of Larry, the only guy any of us knew who had successfully kept afloat a business in the small strip of revolving mom-and-pops for more than six months—that did it. It was a frozen yogurt place—we swarmed there every summer since it's opening three years prior—and we couldn't help but wonder what would become of it now that he'd died on stage.

A few of us wrote our elegies in Facebook posts, tucked into five-star reviews to the Flo's Fro-Yo page, and we remembered Larry's ex wife, who had left town after the divorce when he refused to change the place's name from hers to anything else.

"What if she comes back?" We asked. "We did not like her." We stated.

"Certainly not." We reasoned, in affirmation that we had sided with Larry in the divorce, sympathized with the necessitation of a catchy, recognizable name for the sake of business, and, in conclusion, that Flo would likely not show her face in the town that had quite effectively chased her gone.

We were never afraid to tell others what we thought of them, because in a small town like this, where everyone knows everyone, we had to be selective. People like Larry, who offered excitement and dairy alternatives, were the type of folks we wanted to fill our town with. People like Jess, who owned a consignment boutique specializing in formal attire, and Francine, who always rounded up the carolers for contemporary Christmastime hits, door-to-door.

We knew how hard Jacob, cast in the play as The Head, was taking Larry's death. The two of them were not any closer than we were, in that Jacob frequented Flo's, just like us, but he had been trapped in the horse costume while Larry was beat inside of it, and managed to earn a whack or two himself in the process of laying there, eyes apparently clam-shut. He told us that the sounds and squishes of Larry kept him up at night, so we sent cards, and gift baskets, and casserole, and told him sorry every time we saw him, as though we had committed the crime ourselves and felt bad for drawing him into it. We would never kill Larry though, and we also did not care to know the identity of his killer. We knew we would not like whoever this person was, and when the reporters came asking, we told them that we only wanted the murderer to leave and never return. We simply wanted our town back, and for the news to die down as quick as Larry. After all, it was bad for business.

When many of us were younger, in the time of cropped shirts and sweat-stuck jean shorts, of tan lines and skipping school, we longed for a place like Flo's to blow off steam. There was an ice cream shop back then, Corinne's Cones, but we often got distracted by the owner, Corinne, and her cones, and our ice cream would begin to soup up, cascading over our clenched fists. It never kept as well as our frozen yogurt does now, near impervious to the outdoor seating, walk from shop to car, and the drive home, too. For this reason we envied the youth of our town, for their lackadaisical spreading of limbs and dollars across the grounds of the place, knowing it was superior to the legacy of Corinne's Cones. In spite of this personal, insignificant vendetta, we had been happy for Larry, and we knew how special a place like Flo's was for a town like this.

The frozen yogurt shop was so influential that Larry built on a separate room for events, ranging from birthday parties to business meetings. Book club, knitting circles, Fro-Yo-Yoga, and even funeral receptions came to follow. Graduations, and one wedding, too, had been hosted at Larry's place, and our tongues met every flavor he had to offer over the years.

The wedding between Rodney and Lola came together better than we had expected. Many of the decorations were from the local Bargain Bazaar, tables and doors fettered with twists of orange and pink ribbons hallmarking their favorite flavors—his, raspberry, and hers, orange sherbet. Attendees were ushered to Jess's consignment store and littered the lobby with shades of brown, grey, and black adorning their frames. We knew that the pair of them liked chickens, and, despite the fact that such rural taste was ill-fitting in our rapidly gentrifying town, we bought out the chicken decor and memorabilia at the antiques mall and created a pile of lump-wrapped statuettes, oven mitts, and wall placards. Everyone we liked was there, and we began to take the wedding seriously when Pastor Mark sauntered in only three minutes late, sucking on a curved plastic spoon. We knew, then, all things considered, how much Rodney and Lola loved each other, and how much we loved this place.

Mere weeks after the tragedy made the news, we could

not help but continue to mourn for Flo's Fro Yo, which was meant to open by the end of the month. Although much mystery surrounded the interior of the business ownership and licencing, a notice on one black-framed glass door haunted us with uniform, capital letters cementing our fears that the opening would be delayed. Where else could we spend those extra dollars set aside from our nine to fives in Flo's Fro Yo brand novelty bank jars?

Flashes of that particular night were common to us, around grass-graced patios and in grocery lines, and behind our eyes, too. This was exasperated by the fragmented fire of questions from those who had not attended the play and wanted every gory detail. We practiced our tellings, until it was elevated to nothing short of art.

One moment the horse was standing there, regal in all the ways a rumpled, ill-fitting costume could gleam in the green light cast over the stage. A sound that came from above and behind us clicked to life, summoned a robotic neigh, out of time with the horse's jerky movements across the painted backdrop. There was visible creasing near the bottom of both hooves, which were thick and robust like the trunks of two great trees. This anatomically incorrect design was to conceal the shuffling legs of the sweaty actors cast respectively as The Head and The Ass no doubt, but the scenery really came together, the creases became muscles, and the thready tubes of hair attached at the thing's neck almost began to roll with wind from the rattling air conditioner. The horse had us at that moment, and when it was being beaten to death, we thought about calling, well, someone who deals with animal violence. The ASPCA, maybe? Only after the blood was pooling and we saw glimpses of bruised skin under the sackcloth of the ass did we look around at each other. Some of us went, "oh shit, right," and that's when we called the police.

It was jarring watching the thing that held ransom our disbelief return to piles of cheap, bloody fabric. We wondered if our town would ever be the same. When that white, imposing sign was replaced with another, confirming our most fervent fears, and then a board of wood—once the rocks had shattered bits of glass over Flo's checkered interior floor tile—we knew we would never recover. There was simply nothing left to say.

Illustrations for Award

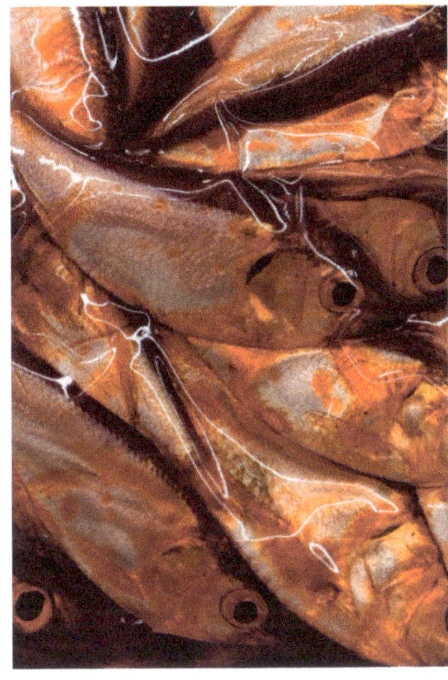

Eyes Clam Shut,
Jes Brockman Artemiev

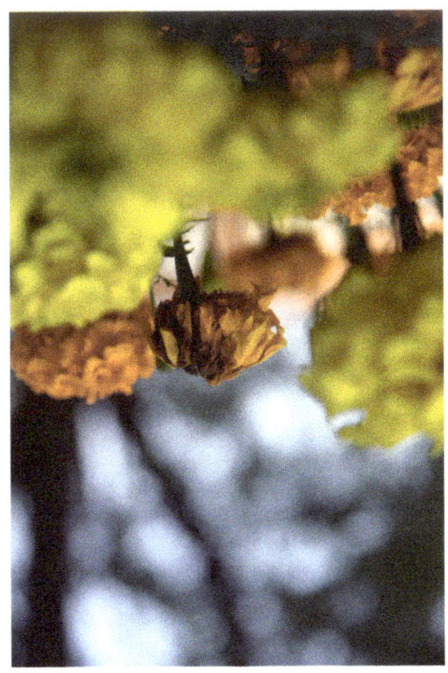

Death Within Life,
Zeke Fredrickson

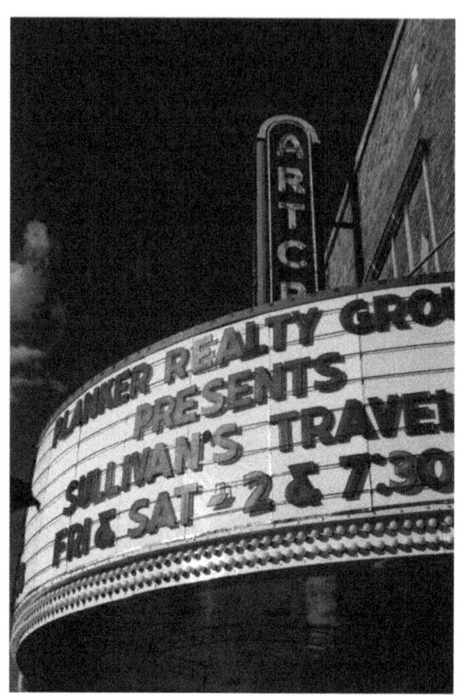

Local Theatre,
Kristen Taylor

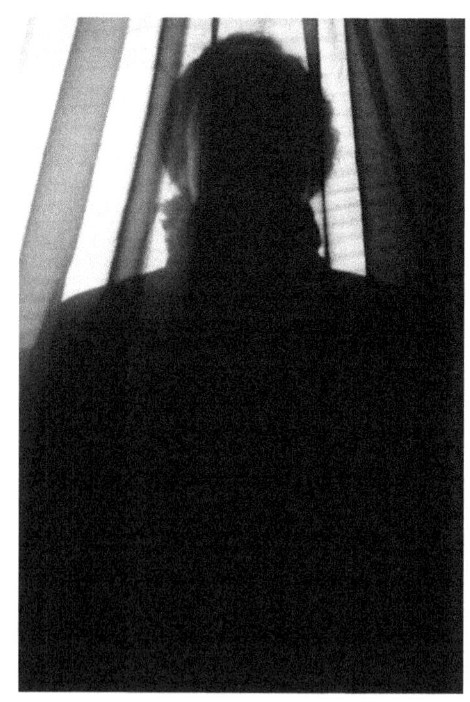

Watcher,
Asiah Avery

Melted Memories, Audrey Kline

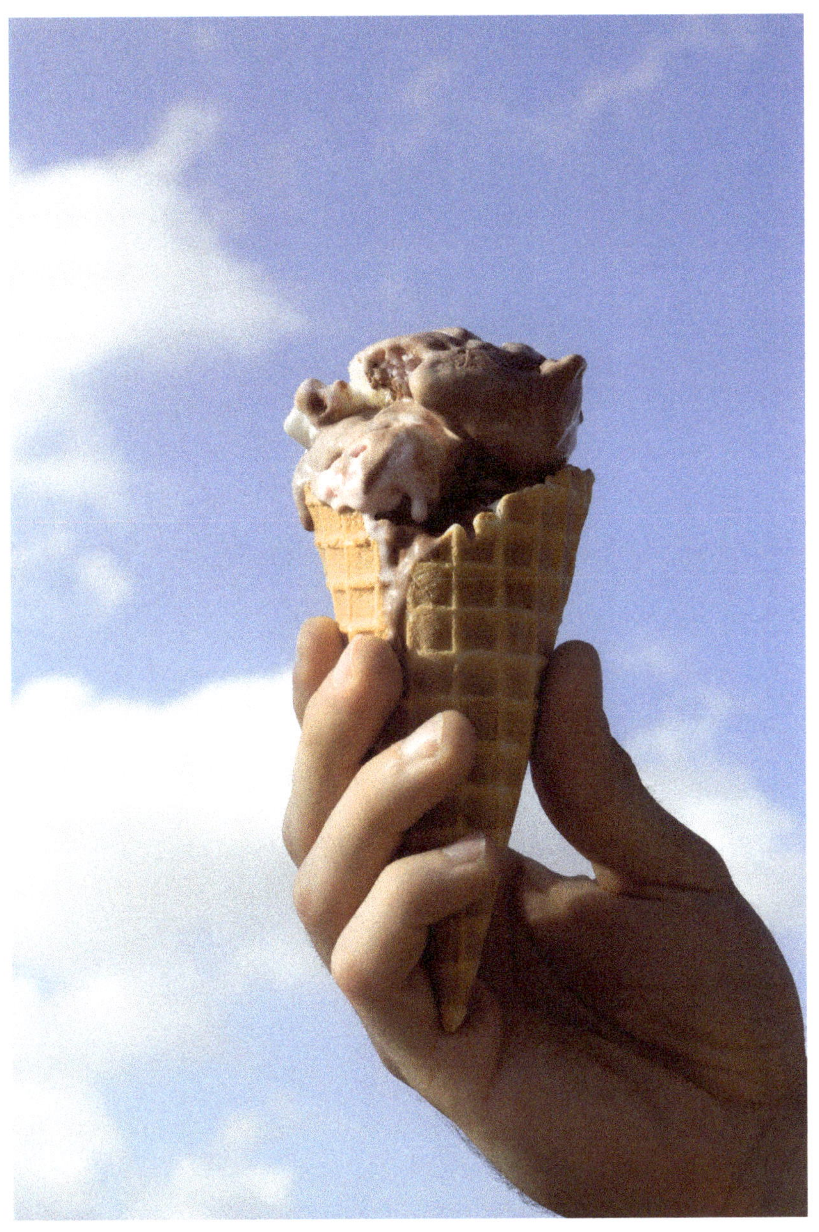

The Curtains Rose

Sierra Durbin

Darling dew
sparkles beneath the spotlights.
She's blooming before the audience,
bursting alive with color.

With whimsical flow,
she charms admirers,
following the rhythm
of wind and song.

Suddenly, the tempo changes.
She sprouts with vivacity and passion,
her determination stemming
from her awakened spirit and love to put on a show.

Caught in a whirl,
spinning in a frenzy,
the silky skirt spirals
and flutters around her body.

Red, but morphing to crimson,
dull, and darkening her hue,
cheeks once flushed, her limbs begin to fall,
drooping, she slowly kneels.

Losing herself,
the animation dies.
And still holding on to life,
she bows at the end of her final performance.

One Day I Updated Spencer's Poem of the Strand

Robert Springer

One day I wrote her name upon the shore,
But waves rolled in and washed away the sand.
I wrote her name upon the sand once more,
But tide rose up and covered all the strand.
Proud man, she said, as if your words could stand
Against the slow decay that's sure to be.
As if you could delay the waters creep and
Stay the tide of time that comes for me.
Not true, I said, I swear the world will see
That you are more than just the name you wear.
Our frames, these feeble houses seem to be
So frail, but not our love, to this I swear.
That day when death has swallowed time and chance
We'll burst death's bonds and so renew the dance.

Childhood

Karina Camacho

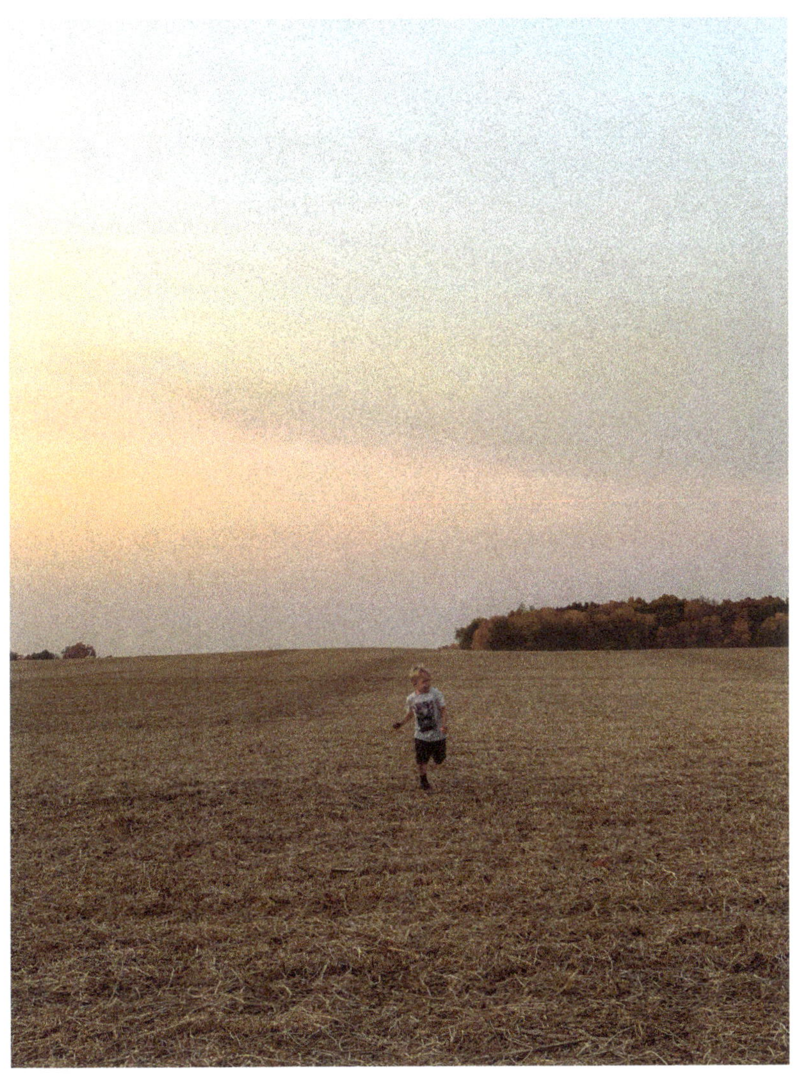

Photograph/Illustration

Photographed in a small town in Indiana fall of 2020. A simple picture but so much more going on behind the camera. The excitement for hayrides and pumpkin patches can be seen through the child.

The Shoe Doesn't Fit

M.J. Loria

Last spring, I spent an afternoon weeding in the garden before a heavy rainstorm rolled in. I worked diligently and swiftly, pulling the clods of weeds from earth surrounding my unkempt hostas. A neighbor glanced over, observing the small piles of tangled weeds that I'd constructed, evenly spread along my brick walkway. I imagined to myself that she was thinking "Finally that shut-in is dealing with the garden. About time." My neighbor's yard is so tidy despite the rest of her life seeming quite the opposite. Appearances are confusing.

I looked to the sky as tumbling clouds sauntered in with a low, continuous growl of thunder echoing behind them. I glanced back down to admire my work and to gather my tools, eager to casually toss them on my rusty porch chair. As I grabbed my trowel, I noticed a small set of eyes looking back at me. A beautiful jumping spider with metallic, bright aqua chelicerae peeking from behind fuzzy, black and white pedipalps.

My heart sank as I realized I'd destroyed his home just before the heavy rains began. I apologized to him. I took a few photos. We studied each other. I wondered why he didn't seem more afraid. It occurred to me that I could find a container that could protect him from the storm and I darted to my china cabinet. I saw the hollow porcelain clog I'd snagged from my grandmother's house last minute, just before she donated what was left. Perfect. He could build a bed in the toe, hidden from everything. The white porcelain would keep the house from getting too hot. My spider friend could have the finest crib in the garden.

Spider was waiting for me when I returned. I carefully nestled the clog on its side near his body. The sky started to spit and I went inside, proud of myself.

A couple of days later, I checked on the porcelain home and Spider was in there! He stretched his way out of a silk sleeping bag he'd built in the sole and peeked his head out to say hello. I felt happy.

More rain came through. And so did some big depression. And then more rain. I didn't check on him for some time. When the day came that I finally went to look, I saw from my porch that the porcelain clog had flipped over in the garden. The opening was flat against the ground. I felt numb.

When I lifted the clog and peeked inside, Spider was shriveled and dead in his sleeping bag. I felt less numb.

I pulled his lifeless body from the prison I'd unintentionally locked him in. I buried his body in the spot I'd first met him. My heart was heavy enough to drown out the numbness. A tear. And then more. Why had I interfered? I cringed when I saw things for what they were. I killed Spider by trying to help him.

I brought the porcelain death chamber inside and placed it next to my coffee pot. Every morning for many months, I looked at the clog while my coffee brewed. I reflected on my mistake; I ached for a chance to go back and do a better job. I grieved for Spider more than I could make sense of.

Over the months, Spider thawed a tiny area of my heart like the first days of spring. And in that space, my pain grew like weeds. I began to recognize that Spider wasn't the only soul I was grieving for. His wasn't the only sweet spirit suffocated by a prison of my creation. Through his death, I found my-*self*: a forgotten child, sweet and gentle, who has been gasping for air for far too long.

Arise My Soul

Chloe Crockett & Heather Dawson

"Arise My Soul" is a song composed to inspire feelings of hope. Amidst each of our struggles and trials, God offers freedom and light. We hope this song brings peace and comfort to the hurting heart.

She IS

Danielle Shaw

She is a line break—
Unexpected, yet necessary, all at the same time
She is following a form—
Yet no set path, as she can break off at any time.
She is a rhyme scheme.
Effortlessly putting something together to make a masterpiece.
Like an Olympic synchronized swimming team.
She is a forever purchase but a short team lease.
She is unique
And
She cannot be made to fit one certain
Genre
Or style.
She is creative,
An original work of art,
Never seen before.
She is like a blank sheet of white paper
Waiting to be covered in bright blue ink
She often repeats line after line.
Often, line after line, she repeats.
She is unlike anything else ever seen
Art is subjective, it can't be ID'd
Writing words and making lines, she is keen
Paper and pens are not wants but are needs
Let her go and see what she can create
She is God, and her words are the planet earth
Building worlds and deciding our fates
Her work is a baby, one she just birthed.
She is constantly pregnant with new work,
Never giving the hand that is her womb
Some time to rest, leaving it red and irked.
Most don't make it, with journals as their tombs
But for a small moment, they were alive
And ink is the way to make some revive
She is free.
She is constantly changing.
She is
Poetry.

Usable Decay

Maiya Johnson

On top of what is left of me lays roses and sunflowers
The lies you told me were sewn in the stitches of my gown
You brushed my hair behind my ear
Before betraying me
You showed me vulnerability
Only to serve yourself
The roses you gave me decay on the counter
You wedged me like clay you thought you'd sculpt me
Into someone *usable*

The Edge of Glory

Riley Childers

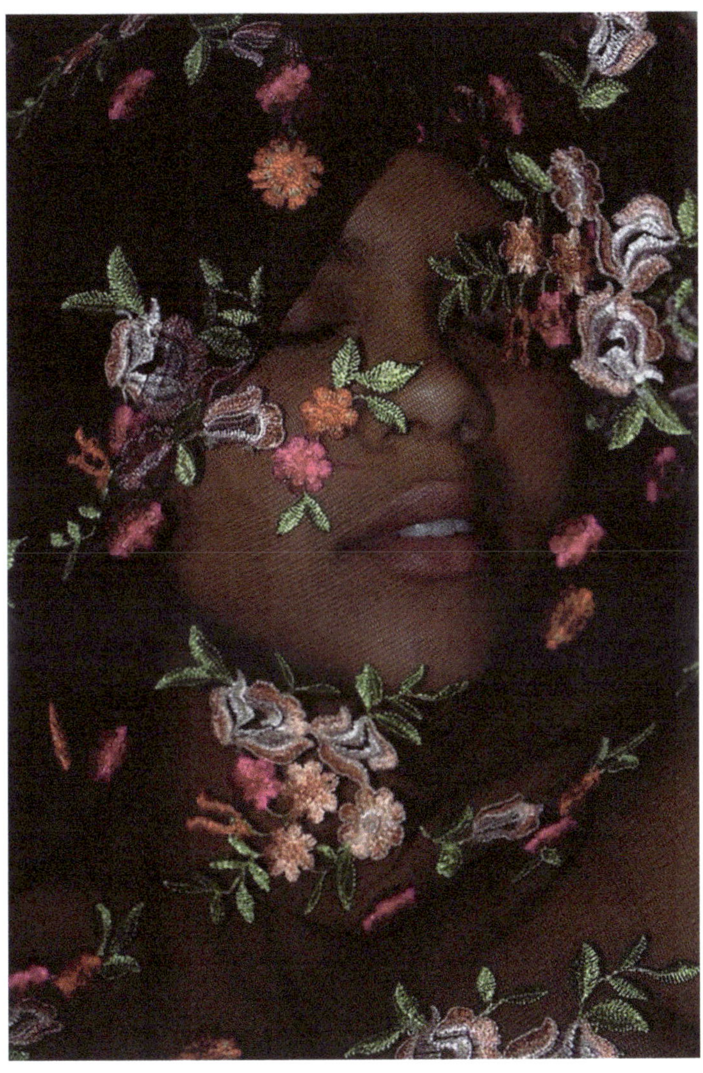

Photograph

This piece is part of an ongoing project called “50 Shades Freed.” This project has allowed me to show different sides of my wonderful friend, CariAnn.

Neon Nights

Sydney Smith

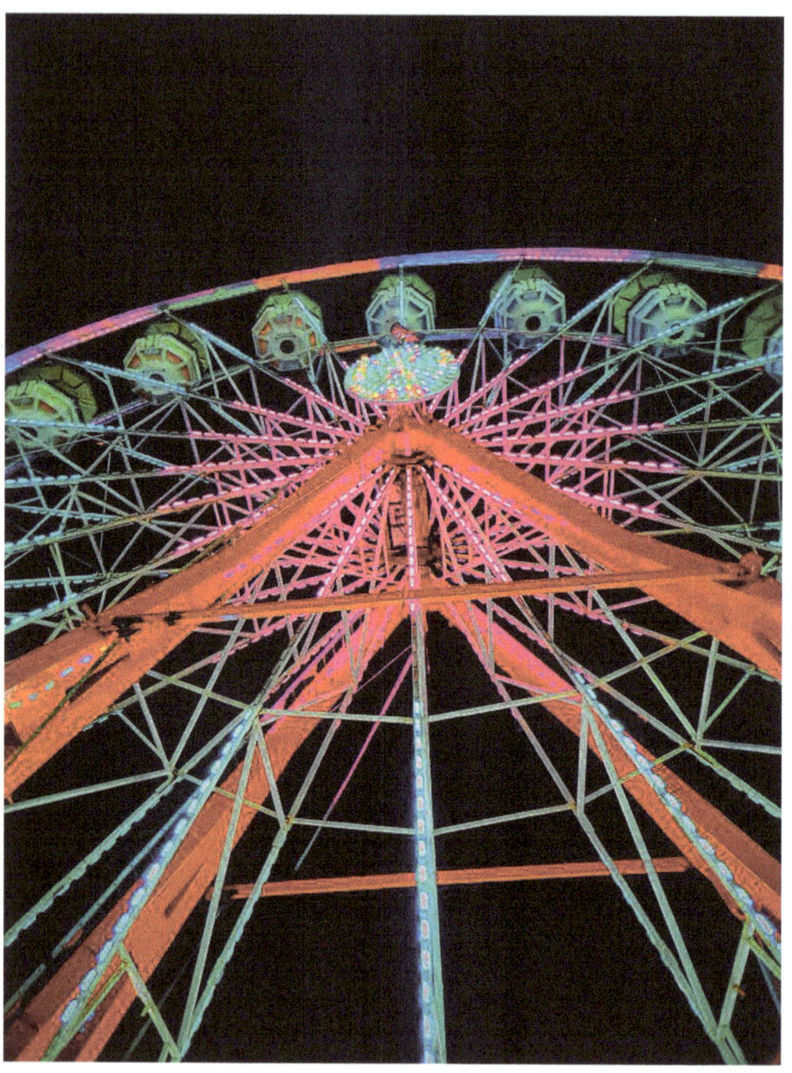

Photograph

This photograph was taken at my hometown's county fair. The contrast of the bright, neon colors against the dark night sky brings me feelings of happiness and excitement, reminding me of the fun I had over the summer.

Broke

Julia Swindeman

It came to me slowly. It started
in my abdomen and was a deep
dark pit. It was dread and disorder and
an absolute disaster.
The questions rise from a place of
insecurity. They are persistent and irritating.
One might say that they are
annoying.
They hurt my head. Sharp. Stabbing.
It makes me a rollercoaster of emotion that
turns into a tsunami. Cut me down, and tear me up
maybe even spit me out. Make me into something
besides what I am and make me into something
insignificant. Let me fade ever so
subtly. Let me disappear into the
dust from which I came.

Lay me down slowly and I will be free
But do not dare raise your voice at me.

Banana

Sydney Nichols

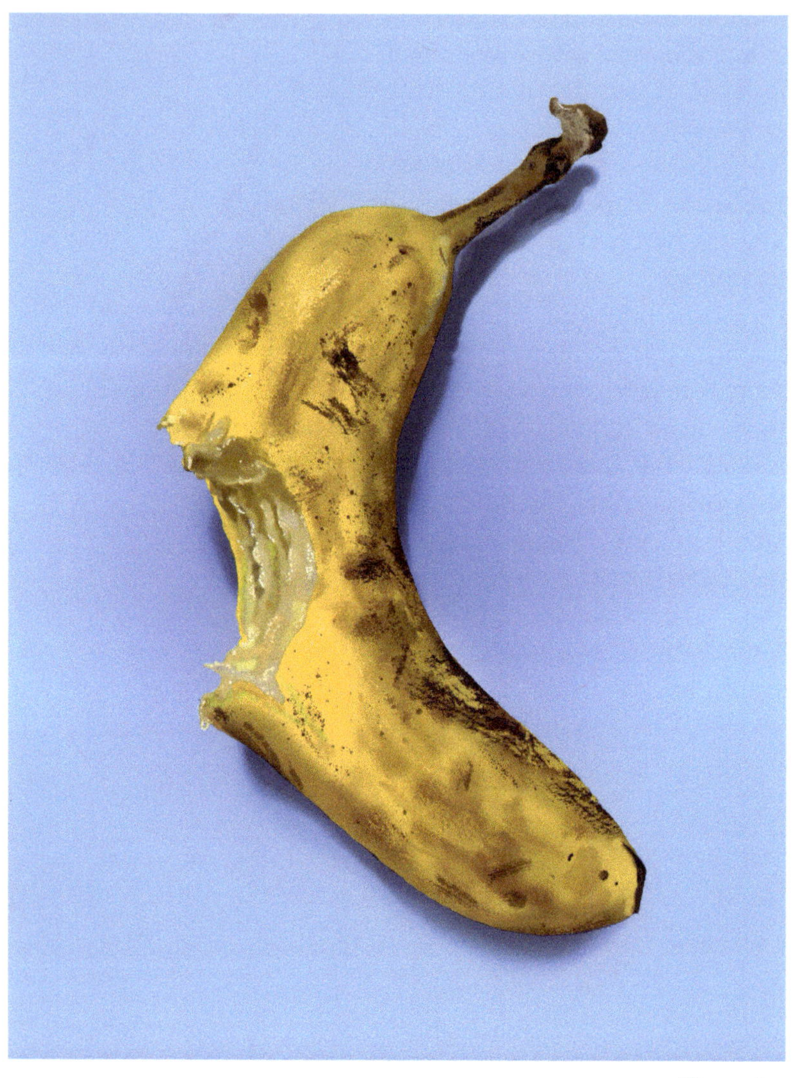

Illustration

I intended for this piece to provoke feelings of discomfort; just as uncomfortable it was to bite a banana from the side for my reference picture. Although, I do find it easy to relate the discomfort to a big life change, like moving to college.

The Princess that Rot in the Tower

Sierra Durbin

Seeming to elevate high into the sky,
the stacks of stone create the spectacular tower.
No one expected life up there,
Surrounded by a garden of thorns.

Trapped in her room hovering above the Earth,
she paced back and forth in her prison.
Biting her lips and ripping at her hair,
the princess begged for someone to listen.

Dressed in moss and armored with vines,
the twisted structure curled up to the heavens,
while its roots dug down into hell,
looming over a path that was hardly even there.

Like a sinister spiderweb,
the tower sat there menacingly
holding down its helpless victim,
forbidding her to escape.

The birds flew by without a care,
not daring to perch at the window.
Squirrels and mice never risked the climb.
Even the insects knew to stay away.

Oh, how she craved even the buzz
of a mosquito in her ear
to fill the silence
of her loneliness.

The day continued to drown the princess
further in her sorrows.
Cheeks burning with a shining smile,
the sun seemed to mock her.

As time passed there appeared
to never be a tomorrow to follow.
Her existence was stagnant
while the world moved around her.

The dance of the fireflies in the night remained enticing,
inviting her to join their fun.
Gazing out the window,
she saw the stars shimmer without her.

Longing for the taste of freedom
to be more than a dream,
the princess felt another piece of her die
as she continued to slowly rot in her tower.

Punk Goblin

Pamela Smith

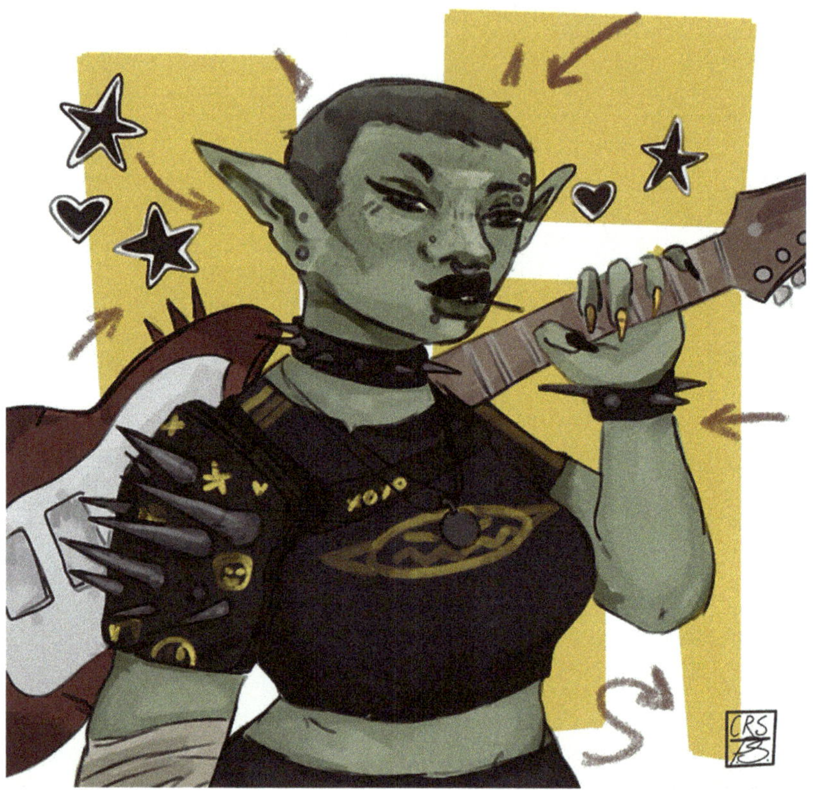

Illustration

This summer I had wanted to focus on my abilities as an illustrator, and found an accidental muse in my dungeons and dragons character. I think I've drawn her more times than minutes spent playing, but I still appreciate her for the help in my growth.

Trashy Food

Nicholas Jackson

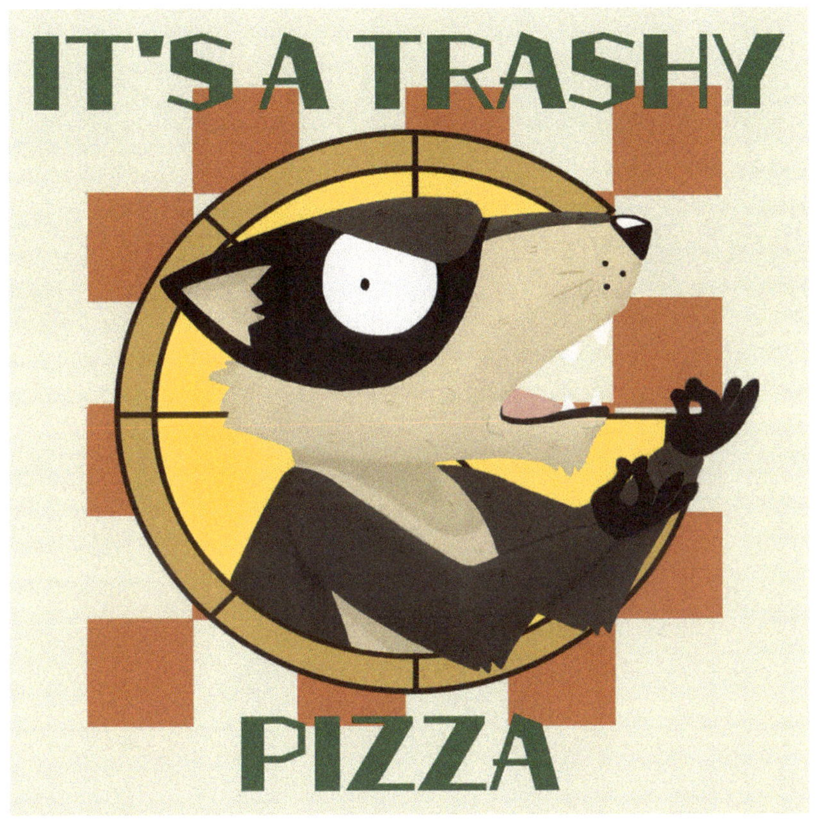

Illustration

We often indulge in unhealthy foods. Life is short. Enjoy it, along with all the foods you love.

Lost in the Past

Cambel Castle

And there I stood on the edge.
Teetering between now and then.
Balancing on the memories,
that seem so far away.

I walk along this cliff often,
debating whether or not to jump,
to fallback.
To get lost in those thoughts.

Somedays I jump.
Somedays I find myself back where I started in seconds,
Other times,
It takes me weeks to find my way.

—cliff jumping.

Free Bird

Mia Lehmkuhl

i have stood
at the precipice
of drawing breath
or losing it

i have walked
to the cusp
of a rocky skyscraper
and managed to turn the other cheek
to its jagged jaws

i have ran
to and from the alluring depths
feeling the tide just barely
sweep me off my feet

nothing's better
than feeling alive
when you are closest to your demise
so as i drag my feet to the edge of the world

for the final time

i lifted my arms
and i flew.

Buried Beneath the Oak Tree

Coda Barger

I would like to die in the woods
Where sound cannot reach my bones
Where my flesh is consumed by the Earth
Because the grass has always been my first love

I would like to rest in the woods
Where the rushing water takes me away
Where dandelions bloom and fairies play
Because the flowers have always felt like home

I would like to lie in the woods
Where monarchs rest their orange wings
Where shadows dance among the trees
Because the butterflies are gentle—unlike other things

The empty farmland is where I'll rest
The blue jays will sing my lament
The woodpecker will be the drums
The worms will hum a quiet tune
While I lay within my tomb

She shall be my eternal resting place
Where chipmunks and foxes run
Where I'll always be free
Because I'd rather be buried
Beneath the big oak tree.

Bone Creeper

Sierra Durbin

CW: Animal death, blood, death, eating disorders

Darkness surrounded the Pearson family RV as they drove down the deserted road. The moonlight was shaded by the blanket of bleak clouds, so the only light source beamed from the headlights. The glow casted into the foggy void. John and his wife, Cindy, sat up front, while their teenagers, Riley and Dylan, sat in the back, leaning into the aisle to make sure their father didn't fall asleep at the wheel. Max, the young Collie, sat on Dylan's lap, periodically licking his face and causing Riley to giggle at his struggle. Little hairs from his fluffy, white fur drifted down his wagging tail. Riley could see the shadow of his black, floppy ears bouncing. Their great aunt was a widow and hermit who lived in a cabin in the woods of Maine. She died a few weeks ago. Their father did not disclose what happened to her body. He volunteered to help clean out the cabin, and thought, despite the morbid circumstances, it was the perfect opportunity to take his family on a fairly relaxing vacation. Overall, the kids did not seem bothered by the situation. Of course they felt sorry for losing a family member, but they did not know their great aunt well enough to shed tears. They could hardly remember the woman's face. The only thing that came to mind was how often she bit her nails and lips. Regardless of the destination, Riley felt like she needed a change of scenery. Her life was overwhelming with college on the horizon, boy drama, and coping with recovery. *I just need an escape, even if it is only for three weeks.* The RV jostled after dipping into a massive pothole, distracting Riley from her thoughts.

"Hey, kids, it feels like we're back in Indiana!" Their father chuckled.

Even with lack of sleep, he still conjured up jokes. A few more miles down the road, the kids began to feel drowsy.

The sea of black swallowed them up, and the rocking of their vehicle lulled them enough to doze. But just as things seemed quiet, an enormous, scraggy figure of flesh scurried across the pavement. Everyone exclaimed in terror in a varied chorus of "What the hell was that?"

"We're by the forest already, so it's most likely a moose," John suggested.

Riley shook her head, "Dad, that looked too tall and skinny to be a moose. That was about 6 feet tall!"

"They can be about that tall," he continued to reassure her.

"No way that bony thing was a moose. It was like a skeleton," Dylan nervously added.

The mother and father glanced at each other briefly.

"You were probably seeing his antlers, honey, and I would bet your eyes are playing tricks on you. This fog is just insane up here." There was no way to convince their mother either.

Riley and Dylan looked at each other, eyes wide and in agreement. *That was no moose...*

***

They arrived at the cabin late in the evening the next day. The songs of cicadas filled the air. Riley hopped out with her phone in position, ready to take pictures. She dabbled in photography because it was the only thing that reminded her to slow down and appreciate the present. Overgrown weeds outlined the dark auburn log cabin. The wood looked drenched due to heavy amounts of rain. The dingy exterior exuded a dank, foul smell of mold like it was tucked in the crevices. An outdoor porch wrapped around the slanted building. Riley carefully stepped and snapped pictures of the decaying dwelling. The place looked unstable as she walked up the creaking, rickety steps. She couldn't imagine her great aunt living there the remaining years of her life. She shivered at the thought of the woman dying within the walls of where she will be sleeping for the next few weeks. Riley returned to the RV to help her family unpack their belongings. After stepping inside, she nearly gagged at the smell of rot and death, "Oh my god, what is that smell?"

"Seems like the place is falling apart and the poor woman couldn't keep up." The father rubbed some dust off a coffee table with his finger...*Disgusting.*

"Woah! Those look wild!" Dylan beamed at the sight of the antique shotguns hanging above the soot-covered fireplace.

"Woah indeed." John joined his son in admiring the weapons. "Hey, keep an eye out for the bullet casing and maybe your old man will show you a few tricks." He jabbed Dylan in the side with his elbow and winked.

The cabin appeared much smaller on the inside. The wood, black from soaking up moisture, resembled an abyss, as it sucked in the light. Furniture was sparce except for the basics. A worn reclining chair hid in the corner of the room by one of the main windows, which appeared to be raised and stuck in place. On the left of the chair was a rusted, brass pull chain lamp. A tall wooden bookcase rested on the opposite side of the chair. Riley gandered through the stacks of tattered books bowing the shelves. They seemed to be organized by category...Zoology, paranormal, supernatural, ancient and fairly current folklore, cryptology...The topics grew more bizarre with each new peak of a cover. *This must be what she did with all of her time.* On the middle shelf, a fairly recent photograph caught her attention. A wrinkly, withered old woman, most likely her great aunt, held two young children on her lap, probably Riley and Dylan as toddlers. If it wasn't for the weight of the two children anchoring her down, the wind might have carried her away. A wave of sadness washed over her while picturing how lonely the woman must have been cooped up in her shack with only stories to keep her company. *What happened to her?*

***

The family decided to visit the nearby town to eat dinner for the night. It was about 20 minutes before they saw any sign of civilization. They drove by some old shops and broken-down houses.

"Man, this place looks abandoned." Dylan's eyes were glued to the window.

They eventually found a diner that was luckily filled with a few people, leaving them hope for the town not being entirely dead. The restaurant looked like it belonged in the 1950s with its shiny, checkered floor and red leather booths. The Pearson family grabbed a booth by a window that faced the only existing gas station.

"I cannot believe this town doesn't have fast food restaurants." Riley examined the old-fashioned diner while munching on a plate of fries, periodically snapping photos that captured the retro aesthetic.

"That is somewhat surprising. I guess they assume there isn't enough traffic around here." Cindy shrugged and then continued to point out the different pieces of décor.

"I'm just glad you're eating again." John playfully poked his daughter's nose with a French fry.

***

Moon and stars took over the sky by the time they arrived back to the cabin. Engulfed by shadows, the cabin appeared less welcoming than before. Their father encouraged sleeping in the cabin so everybody could get what he referred to as "the experience." Everyone stood outside of the RV, almost as if waiting to see who was brave enough to walk up first. The dad pulled out a flashlight and lit his path up the creaky steps to the front door. Max greeted him, wagging his tail as always. Dylan lured him outside to potty. As soon as he ran onto the dirt-covered ground, he started growling and barking towards the cluster of trees.

"Hey, what are you barking at, Boy?" Dylan tried grabbing at Max's collar but he wouldn't stand still.

The dog kept inching forward and then backing away with a whimper like something was taunting him in the dark. Riley, leaning in the entrance of the front door, peered into the darkness trying to search for whatever troubled Max. She decided to yell, "Do you see anything?"

"I don't see a damn thing!" Dylan sounded annoyed.

Riley would be too if she didn't feel so anxious. A shadow seemed to move in the distance. She lifted her phone and took a picture with flash, accidently blinding her brother.

"Jeez, Riley. Ya could have given me a warning." He blocked his face with his hand.

"Sorry. I thought it might catch something we don't see but Max does." She turned to follow her brother inside and realized the barking ceased.

"Max?"

No bark, not even a whimper. Just silence.

"Max??" Riley's voice raised with more concern.

She couldn't see anything in front of her besides splotches of light from her flash bopping in the dark. She hollered for her brother and parents to help her look for him. Sound seemed amplified out in the woods, from the nighttime orchestra of the crickets and frogs to the whistles and wails of the hysteric family.

"If he doesn't show up in the morning, you guys can try printing off some pictures of Max at the library. It's getting late and I think I felt some raindrops." Cindy wrapped her arms around her kids. "Don't worry. We'll find him." Their heads dropped in disappointment. After stepping inside, both Riley and Dylan pointed out an odd red splotch on their mother's face. She wiped her finger across her cheek and studied the spot of blood, her eyes wide as saucers.

***

That night, Riley struggled to sleep on her blow-up mattress in the living room. Dylan's presence was slightly comforting as he slept close by on his airbed, but she couldn't stop worrying about Max. He seemed to vanish in thin air. Her brother looked restless so it must have bothered him too. She pulled out her phone to scroll through the images she took earlier, one of them being the flash in the dark. She squinted and saw the shadow of a lanky humanoid figure crouched in the distance. The voice of her mother echoed in her ears, "Your eyes are playing tricks on you." *No. Max saw something.* The wind howled outside, like an animal. The sound chilled

Riley to the bone.

***

Dylan and Riley woke up extra early. Not only did they hardly sleep a wink, they also wanted to post as many flyers as possible before lunch. With the help of daylight, their parents decided to stay at the cabin to continue looking for Max. The siblings unpacked their bikes from the RV and raced into town. Luckily, the library was easy to spot because it was one of the oldest buildings that were still functional. The two walked out of the ancient brick structure with a stack of pictures of Max. They stopped by a small store to grab the supplies they needed to hang the photos. Split up, like people never should do in horror movies, they biked around, stapling flyers on poles. Riley pedaled by another dinky store and noticed a small group of sickly teenagers that looked as thin as she once did. They seemed drained, like they were barely clinging to life as they swayed unsteadily. The image brought back memories. She tried shaking them away, but it only made her feel dizzier. Moments later, Riley spotted Dylan and pointed out visiting the coffee shop. A bell rung above them as soon as they opened the door. A nice young woman greeted them, "Hello, may I help you?"

"Yes," Riley felt her voice tremble a little, "Would you mind if we posted a flyer of our lost dog? He went missing last night."

"Oh, of course, and I'm so sorry to hear that." Her sweet voice sounded sympathetic.

"Thank you. We appreciate it."

Just before they walked out of the building, an old woman in the corner caught their attention.

"Did you say you lost your dog?" Her voice was raspy like she choked on gravel and needed to clear her throat.

"Um, yes. Could you keep an eye out?" Riley walked over and handed her one of the flyers.

"Ah, yes, lovely dog...reminds me of a fine lab that went missing a month ago, and a terrier just a while before that..." The old woman sipped her coffee casually, a strand of her scraggly white hair nearly slipping into her drink.

"Oh, that's awful. Were they ever found?" Riley glanced at her brother, worried.

"No, the owners never saw them again. They must have been little snacks for the Bone Creeper..." Just then she took a bite of the crispy biscuit that sat next to her cup.

"Little snacks for the what?" Dylan repeated questioningly.

"The Bone Creepers are infamous around here and have been ever since I was a little girl. Large animals and people have gone missing over the years. They've caused a lot of paranoia in the folks, the young ones especially. Many of them have turned to anorexia in hopes the Bone Creepers would stay away because they lack meat on their bones. It is quite the talk around here for the remaining residents who haven't disappeared or straight up left."

Dylan shot a glance at his sister before commenting, "Wow, that's crazy. I wonder if that's what we saw on our way up here. Dad swears we saw a moose." He lightly laughed in disbelief.

"A moose? Hell, we haven't seen a moose or even bears in ages."

The siblings thanked the old woman and left the shop even more worried about their dog.

Bone Creepers...Missing animals and people...Causing anorexia...What the heck was going on in this town? It sure as hell wasn't a moose.

***

Riley couldn't shake this feeling that she was being watched as she walked up those shaky steps. She turned around, expecting to see a person, a spirit, a *Bone Creeper.* The only thing that greeted her was the silence of the forest. The lack of sound bothered her. Then a loud crack of a stick from inside the canopy of leaves interrupted the quiet, prompting Riley to practically jump out of her skin. Dylan laughed, causing her to jump again

"Calm down, sis. Don't listen to that lady's kooky old

legend."

Other people in the town believed the existence of the Bone Creeper was real, but no one had ever actually seen the creature and lived.

***

Later in the evening, Riley and Dylan planned to walk around the woods in search of Max. They brought his favorite treats in hopes that the smell would entice him out of his hiding place. The sky was somewhat dreary and they worried if they wandered too far that they would be caught in the rain. They ventured long enough for their legs to feel weak and their stomachs start to grumble.

"I hate to say it, but we should probably start to head back." Dylan sighed in defeat.

Riley's heart ached because she knew how much it hurt him being separated from his best friend, and eating was the last thing on her mind.

"Wait. I think I hear something!" Riley stopped in her tracks and motioned for Dylan to do the same. She tilted her head to listen...Drip, drip, drip. She followed the sound and Dylan followed her. The dripping grew louder with each step forward...Drip, drip, drip. It was the only sound that seemed alive because everything around them fell silent. A thick, gooey mucus saturated the surrounding plant life. Dylan poked it with a stick and moved the unnatural substance, until it sunk into the slime. Riley took a photo, the sludge glistening in response to the flash on her phone. They stumbled upon a large tree dripping drops of crimson, smacking the large ferns below. Their eyes slowly trailed up the bark. Gasps caught in their throats. They were disturbed to the point of gagging. Tangled up in the tree was the wickedly sprawled corpse of their dog, or what was left of him. His stomach was sliced gruesomely up to his chest, leaving his intestines to dangle and drip with blood. The once soft coat was now matted with a mixture of blood, mud, and ooze. Riley felt her skin start to feel clammy like she was going to faint. The brother and sister clung to each other as they stumbled back to the cabin.

With tears in their eyes, they struggled to keep the other from collapsing. After staggering inside, Riley immediately dropped to the floor, wailing over the macabre sight. Their parents rushed in panic to ease their distraught children. Neither Riley nor Dylan could explain without choking up or nearly vomiting. Man's best friend was also a monster's best victim.

Animals go missing when the Bone Creeper is near...People disappear too.

***

The past few sleepless nights, Riley replayed the horrific sight of their dog's corpse in her nightmares. Like old film footage, blurred and crackling, the death of her aunt played in her mind. The woman's eyes nearly popped out of her head while a razor-sharp claw sliced open her stomach. The gnarly finger trailed up her gaping wound, slashing her throat, just in time to block her scream. The scene ended as soon as Riley woke up in the middle of the night, drenched in sweat and startled by the tree limbs shaking in the breeze. She peeled the covers off of her sticky skin and peaked out the window, paranoid that something was watching her. She felt eyes stare at her, camouflaged by the compact vegetation. She continued to watch until her eyes burned and begged her to try and let them rest. Dylan woke up, alarmed by the shadow of his sister obsessing at the window. He gaped at her gaunt figure. The outline of her shoulder blades protruded with each inhale.

"Riley?"

She jumped before climbing back into bed.

***

Riley's family was worried about her relapse, and they were not comfortable venturing into town without her.

"Are you sure you wouldn't feel safer tagging along with us?" Her mother tried to persuade her, but her daughter insisted on staying behind.

"I don't want to go *out there.*"

Riley was too afraid to step foot on the grounds that the Bone Creeper roamed at night. He ruled the forest. He controlled the town. *Any place is a trap and there is no escape.*

Her leg shook while sitting in the old reclining chair in the dark living room, impatiently waiting for her family to return. It felt like the musky odor burned the hairs in her nose as it lingered in the air. She recalled the last words that her mother emphasized before finally shutting the door, "We'll be quick." As soon as they left, she rushed around the cabin and turned off all the lights so she wouldn't draw attention to herself. Time ticked slowly. Exhausted from the lack of sleep, she teetered on the edge of dozing until she snapped back into reality. She heard a growl outside of her family's cabin. The growl which sounded like the gurgle of the hungry beast. She peaked out the window curtains to see if she could spot where it was and noticed the rustle of the bushes in the woods. A massive, skeleton-like body crept through the moist moss and tangled vines. The greenery was covered in a thick mucus, probably from its slobbering mouth. The skin stuck to the bones like a drink pouch sucked tight, leaving the ribs and collarbone to protrude. Its limbs were warped like spindly spider legs, except this creature only had two arms and two legs...like a human...a 7-foot human...The girl stared in terror, eyes unable to blink. She slightly shifted to the side to watch the wretched thing continue its path through the darkness. The floorboards creaked. Stopping in its tracks, the beast whipped its head around, revealing bulging, black eyes, and a dangling mouth full of fangs. It stared at the cabin, its eyes fixated on the girl. She felt frozen...from the cold that seeped through the cracked window and from the fear settling within her. She blinked. The gnarly thing rushed towards her. She struggled to shut the window. THUMP—CREAK. Riley couldn't tell if she was hearing the creaking of the window or the cracking of the cryptid's bones. THUMP—CREAK. The window was stuck in place. THUMP—CREAK. *Come on...* THUD. The window finally shut just as the monster smacked into it, the force pushing Riley to the ground. She stared up at the sickening silhouette surrounded by pale moonlight. Its dilated eyes made her skin itch. She shivered while watching it calculate the situation. It trailed its boney 12-inch finger across the glass, outlining her figure. Its claws screeched the surface like metal scraping a porcelain plate. It was hungry, she knew. And it wanted her. She felt helpless as she watched it use its upper limb as a bat and shatter the window. Creeping through like a spider, it crawled its way towards her. *If only we found those bullets...*Crouched, it hovered over her. She stared up at its thick, bulbous eyes. It traced its bony finger from her stomach, up to her throat, and stopped at her trembling lips, before opening its mouth wide.

Shadow

Destini Mink

My shadow follows me.
One foot after another.
One step after the first.
One nervous tick after the next.
It follows each motion,
Lifeless,
Mindless.

The sun is particularly high today, it's noon.
My shadow is almost gone.
It's hiding today.
It doesn't like the sun.
It prefers the dark,
I guess we're more alike than I thought.
She's fearful.
Concealed.

Today it's cloudy.
I haven't seen my shadow at all.
Not even a slight glance.
Not one mirrored motion.
Is she okay?

My shadow came back today.
Boldly she followed on the pavement just as she had done before.
I glance around me, and she does the same.
Every other shadow, mirroring their source, as far as the eye can see.
We were no exception.

I glanced down at her, and naturally she glanced up at me.
We were mirroring everyone else.
Lifeless,
Mindless,
My shadow follows me.

Moonless

Mary Redman

After dark, I wandered barefoot
across the lawn in hopes to see
your storied light upon the grass
and threading through the leafy trees.

Instead, dark dampness greeted me,
the scent of earth alive with growth
and waning warmth of an April night.
Only the streetlights cast their glow,
and airplanes dashed like winking stars,
but I never saw that silver sheen
that turns the darkness into day and casts
steep shadows across the ground.
I never found that elusive orb
to inspire my weary, tongue-tied song.

Deliverance

Mia Lehmkuhl

CW: Assault

i stole something
from the heavens itself
i grasped an angel by her wings
and dragged her down to Adamah

as we fell from grace
she clawed the air
hoping to catch even the slightest breeze
in between crushed feathers

i clutched her close
until her shallow breaths thundered church bells into my ears
and her shrieks opposed the trumpets of revelation
sounding in alarm to her sudden absence

i confess
this is no task of the devil
just a selfish man
in an even more selfish world

i sought out purity
and ripped it out of her
i snaked my hand down the base of her neck
seizing beads of dew on my fingertips

her body writhed
in desperation
to exorcise her of my possession

as i traced a finger
delicately down the parted sea of her breasts
her heart thumps against the wood and nail
rivaling the fury of Abaddon himself

after what had been done
the trumpets sounded no more
for her wings lay dead beside her
and her halo fell in gleaming shards at her lap

i left her there
in the revelations of my deeds
then i put on my Sunday best
and fastened my clerical collar.

Candles

Olivia Cameron

snuffed out

God created women
by striking a match.

women are dancing flames;
their bodies wicks,
dripping with sweat,
smelling of vanilla and cedar.

men stick out their noses,
taking a sniff and licking their lips.

they praise the scent,
like the way it makes them
hungry, starving.
they stick their fingers out,
poking at the heat.

oh how they flinch,
when they feel the burn.

they yell
that they hate vanilla and cedar
and the way flames pirouette
around their thighs
as hot wax drips off their hand.

they snuff out
the fire God started.

bite me, i'm burning

that girl is a candle.
i'm addicted to the smell,
sharp sugary sex...
i light her up, watch her burn!
she undulates in the marigold
like the witches of old.
her wax starts to melt
into that sticky, fragrant liquid.
i feel it on my fingers,
skin burning with her scent...
quickly blow her out!
the candle in front of me,
the wick and white, slick inside
reminded me of the apple core
that eve left behind.
adam kissed the juice off her lips,
I would have taken a bite!

Am I on Fire?

I don't always feel like a person.

A planet in space,
a cloud in the sky,
a head without a body.

Why did God make us?
Why do we have minds, hearts, bodies?
We can't truly share any of it.

I can't let you crawl in,
even when I open up
on a page.

You're just reading.

You can't feel me.
And sometimes I can't feel me, either.
my heart beats and breath flows,
but my skin doesn't tingle
with vitality.

Sometimes I feel so alone
that I need to burn.

I'll stick my finger
as close as I can
to the flame of a candle.

To be that close to burning,

When someone has to fix me,
when someone has to kiss my charred skin,
and blow out the flame
I know I am loved.

I'm supposed to let God fill up the emptiness
to know I'm real because he made me so.

I can't hear his voice.

But I can feel flames.

Sparked

Riley Childers

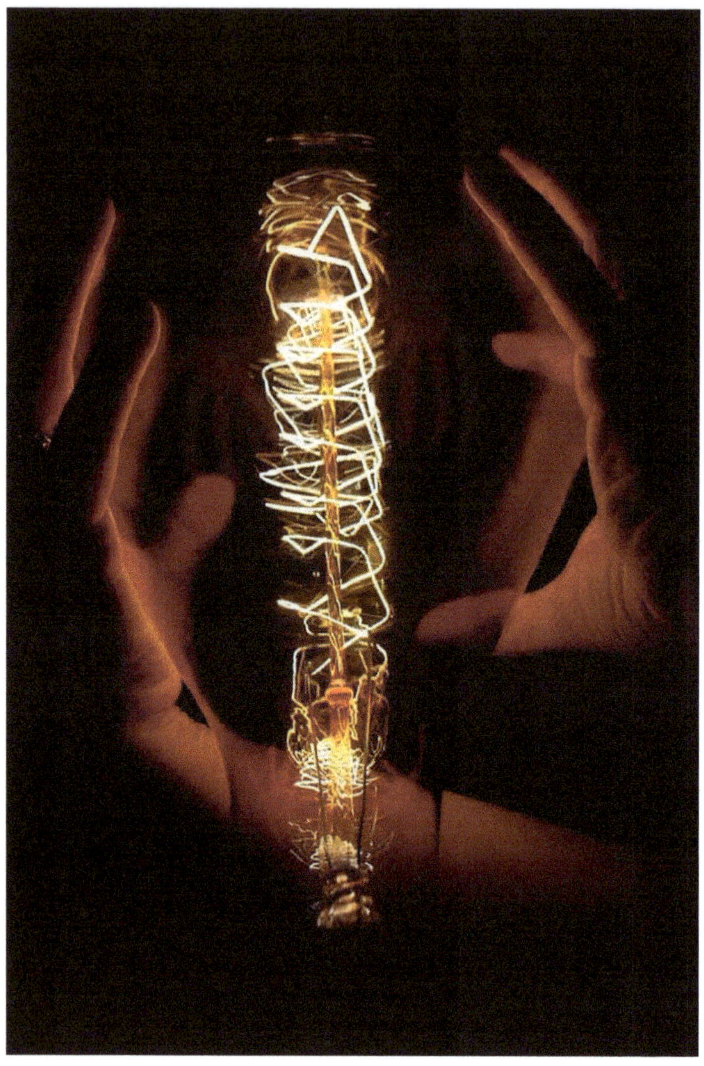

Photograph

“Sparked” is one of my favorite photos because how different and intriguing the lightbulb itself turned out. I’m always drawn to this photo in particular because of the contrast between light and dark.

Wandering Thoughts

Cambel Castle

Have you ever wondered what the wind whispers about?
After all,
it does collect your secrets.
The ones you whisper through tears after dark.
The ones you didn't think anyone would hear.
The wind sprinkles them over the world like fairy dust.
Sharing them with everyone.
So,
maybe think about the gossiping wind,
before you whisper at night.

—it's always listening.

Mother Nature II

Ali Viewegh

"I love you,"
The wind whispered to me.
I will love you even after time breaks.
The Earth will shatter and shake,
Cracks running through the ground,
Fire shooting up.
The essence of space will fracture,
Blinking out of existence.
The moon will come crashing down
Into its once powerful waves.
The sun, so powerful and bold,
Will cease to shine.

Through all of this,
I will still love you.
I will love you for eternity,
After eternity is long over,
And past the end of time.
I will love you until you can take no more,
Then heal you up with the love I have to offer.
Know that I will never stop loving you,
Even as life itself ends
And we have nothing left to hang on to.
Love, I tell you, will live on.

Sky Baby Crybaby

Armani Stewart

The pitter patter of the sky's glistening tears against my window
becomes the soothing sound of my mechanical senses

The sky's glimmering cries sets the mood of tranquility one can't deny,
yet ironically grows the weeping feeling of loneliness; the kind that lingers and whispers to the
silent sheep that sleeps late at night in the protective embrace of its smooth white pillowy sheets

The dripping of the sky's translucent drops against the glassy pane instills a rhythmic lullaby that
has lingering echoes, the deafening screech of its electrifying roar ringing and raging across the
atmosphere, for all of the world to hear

The sky's dauntless outcry succumbs to a gloomy end
Embarrassed, it begins to blush rays of fluorescent color, pigmented into its blue-grey skin,
reflecting in its tear-filled puddles it left behind

The Keyhole

Catherine Platter

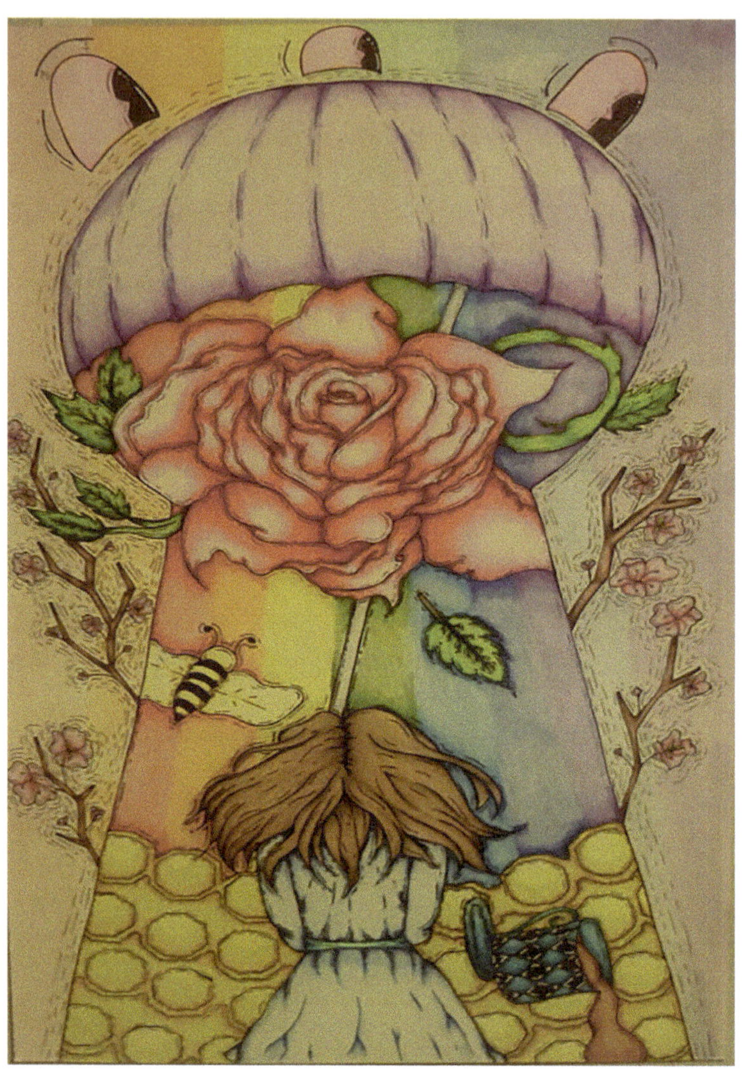

Illustration

"The Keyhole" is a piece made up of symbols typically seen in ideas of "Wonderland" or fantasy worlds. It was created based on the ideas of escaping into a fantasy world and how even things in our everyday can be seen in a fantastical light.

Botany

Mackenzie Hyatt

I have learned
to be less like the fern,
Mimosa pudica,
folding my fronds at a touch,
silent bipinnate applause.

I am now
more like a venus flytrap,
Dionaea muscipula,
offering nectar through
great soft fangs, interlocking.

I know that I am
ancient like the maidenhair tree,
Ginkgo biloba,
with a lineage of mitochondrial mothers,
before there was a word for mothers.

I realize that I am
brand new like the wild ginger,
Hexastylis finzelii,
immature and largely unknown
but a moment in the terrestrial eye.

I love
like the blood-red amaryllis,
Hippeastrum reginae,
stubborn and simple and loud,
a perennial, never prodigal son.

Water me, and I will grow.
Don't, and I may still grow.

Hydrangea macrophylla serrata

Mackenzie Hyatt

When I finally meet you,
perhaps I will call you
my hydrangea, and promise

that I will give you all of the water you
desire and I will keep you
in the sun for as long as I can and

watch you when the sun leaves and
while you sleep, warding off the
deer who might snack on your stems.

And I will feed you fruit above all,
and you will delight in the colors of them,
and I might blanket them in sugar as a treat.

And, with any fortune, you will be my macrophylla,
my mophead.

Your hair will explode like a sunburst atop your sweet head,
and you will be annoyed by its untamability,
but lucky for you, it will not hang limply like mine,

and you will not get bored of it.
But you will get bored of me.
I think that you will, but even if you do,

I won't get bored of you.
Not ever.
And I will remind you what Hydrangea means:

to the Greeks, it meant water barrel,
the same one you could no doubt fill with the tears that will come
when you scrape your knee (because you will inherit my sensitivity)

but I will tell you
it simply means that your heart is full,
and I will refill your barrel anytime you need it.

If I overwater you, please forgive me.

A Vicarious Flight with the Falcon

Mary Redman

who lives in a hollow tree may
open the eyes of a vigilant witness
to a writhing world below.

A swan returns to find his nest
coyote-wasted, a ruined mate
and looted eggs—no cygnets
will survive this spring.

An opossum slinks from shrub
to shed, where dead things feed her
young, sweeps a rat-like tail
and takes a brazen walk in high sun.

Branches hang with season's hue,
but earth lies untidy with leavings
of each past season, its growth,
its gleaning, and all its bitterest gloom.

My fire flickers in a fearsome wind
that threatens light and warmth
'til an upward arc of wide-spread wings
calls me to follow this bird

who has taught herself to hunt
and glide toward an uncertain sky.
With face upturned, I mark her
journey, open my wings, and fly.

King of the Ocean

Sydney Smith

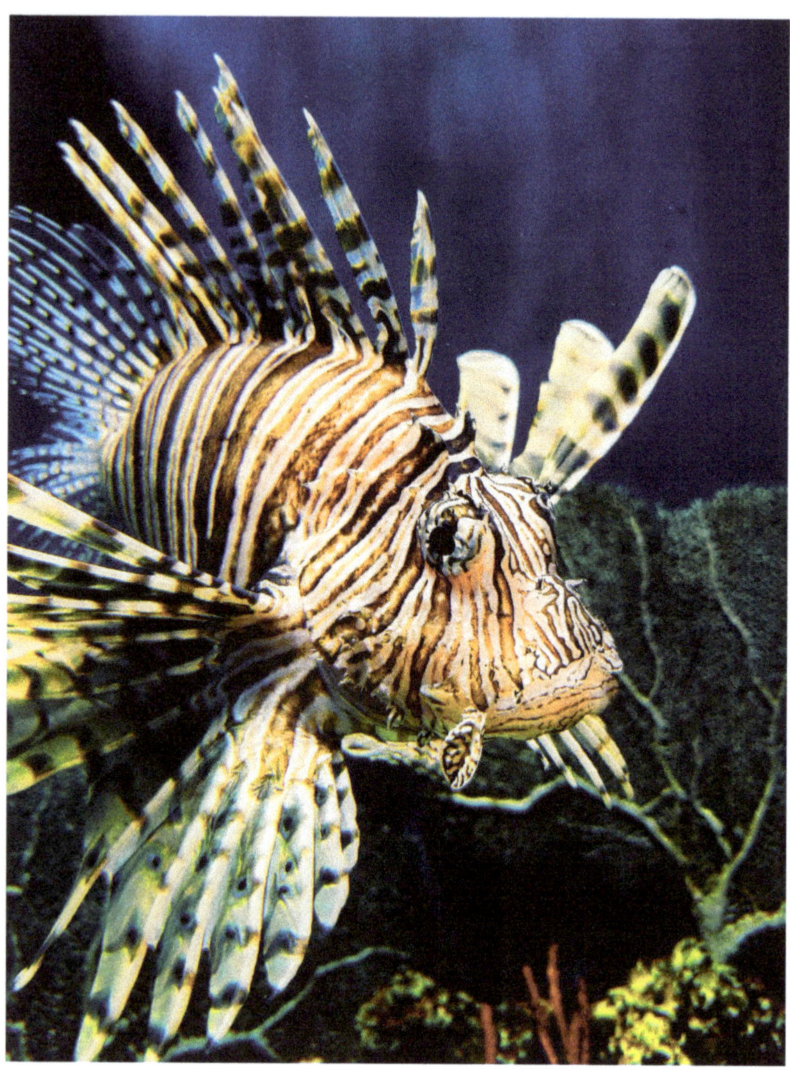

Photograph

Like a lion, the Lionfish is the king of its home, being a top predator of its ecosystem and having a "mane" of its own. This photograph was taken close to UIndy, as it was taken at the Indianapolis Zoo!

The Glass Window

Sydnie Foster

Divided by a glass window, Me and You.
One side is pure blackness, the other a wonderful view.
Pressed up against it, we stand face to face.
One of Us the magnificent view, the other a disgrace.

The blackness only starts as a blanket in the back.
Which seems defeat-able; inexistent, we both just laugh.
Eyes so fixated, Us our only views,
Time diminishes that, creating nothing but rage and blues.

The blackness now covering, strangling around my neck.
The window unbreakable, not even a hidden path to trek.
On the ground now, too weak to even stand.
The only thing You can see, is the palm of my bloody hand.

Pain and sorrow within You, guilt and anger too.
What more could You have done; always an "I love you."
You say this as I scream and curse at You to leave.
Confused on what to do, how to feel, and what to believe.

I watch You walk away, I understand that it's my choice
If I could break the window down, I'd say this using my voice:

"Please believe me when I say, there is no in between
I feel like I'm in a desert full of nothing but two extremes.
I can't control my emotions; I don't know when I will blow,
They are a part of this blackness that continues just to grow.
I don't know when I'll hate You or when I'll think You are the best,
I don't even know when I'll be triggered or become angry, empty, and depressed.
I want to love You the right way, the way that You deserve,

but I don't even love myself, something everyone has observed."

My BPD is part of the window that traps Me alone inside,
And keeps the blackness growing, a reoccurring suicide.
These emotions I get randomly are the opposite of calm,
They explode around my body like an activated nuclear bomb.

These emotions You cannot feel or see, as we sit back to back
Against the glass window, You gave up on wishing that it will crack.
No longer are we looking in each other's eyes,
Too exhausted to give anymore, Your body now paralyzed.

The window stays standing, dividing Us apart.
I know there's a fracture somewhere, I'm hoping with all my heart.
Fully emerged in the darkness, I no longer can see You.
I only pray you're still there because You're my favorite view.
My love for You is stronger than the darkness engulfing me,
You're the better half, I just wish I could make the darkness leave.

What Boyfriends Do

Brandon Hickey

CW: Rape and Sexual Assault

My car slid down the wet country road in the middle of the night. We were returning from a weekend trip to the nearby city. The rain smashed down onto the windshield in tiny puddles and was wiped away by screeching window wipers. Back and forth the wipers went, fighting an uphill battle with the rain. The tires did their best to keep from sliding on the slick asphalt road. It was the middle of the night and the moonlight barely managed to penetrate the thick clouds. Outside the car was the gentle pitter-patter of the rain and the quiet chirping of distant crickets.

I sat behind the wheel. My boyfriend, Wesley, slept in the seat next to me. I quickly glanced at him. I still felt numb from what just happened. Why did I let him do it? Wesely had been waiting for it and honestly so had I, but something just hadn't seemed right. Maybe it was the location? Or maybe I was just tired? But this is what kids my age do, why didn't I want to? I glanced over at Wesley, at his soft, dirty blond hair. Why did I do it?

We were returning from a trip to Little Rock for Labor Day weekend. We spent the weekend there staying at a Best Western. We visited the Arkansas Art Center because I love art and plan on studying it in college. We got to see the drawings of Will Barnet, my favorite artist. My favorite is "Boy Reading" I love the simplicity of it. Its minimalist use of black and white, it was simple, not complex. Something about that spoke to me. I also like the way Barnet creates such a character, the boy is hunched over the book. Is he hiding from someone? Is he trying to forget something? Or is it just a really damn good book? I could stare at the painting for hours and wonder who this boy was and why he buries his face in a book.

Wesley liked "Lifestudy" a drawing of a naked man from behind. Though, something told me it wasn't for its artistic quality.

After the art museum we visited Dickey-Stephens Park to watch the Arkansas Travelers play. I don't care much for baseball, but Wesley loved it and I loved seeing the excited look on his face whenever they hit the ball. The way he smiled and his blue eyes went wide. I loved his blue eyes.

We spent some time walking around and looking at the shops. It was getting late and we decided to head back home, but on the way we passed a lake and Wesley had me stop. He told me to pull into a secluded spot by the shore. Wesley got out and approached the water, taking off his shirt.

"What are you doing?" I asked as he ran towards the shore.

"Going for a swim." Wesley answered while taking off his shoes.

"You don't have a swimsuit."

"Don't need one." Wesley unbuttoned his shorts and stood there in his boxers. Wesley was, in my humble opinion, the cutest boy I'd ever seen. Wesley's body was very pleasing to the eye, he was a swimmer so he was fit but not too fit. Some muscles but some softness too. I was lucky to have him. My body is fine but it isn't much to look at. My muscles aren't defined and I have a bit of fat on my stomach. Wesley says it's cute but I don't believe him. I don't really like thinking about my body, it bums me out.

"You're insane!" I laughed. "It's the middle of the night. It's probably freezing." Wesley ran into the water until it was up to his belly button.

"Come on!" Wesley motioned towards me. I shook my head and smiled.

"It's not that cold!" Wesley said. I kept shaking my head. If he thought I was going to strip down and swim in a freezing lake then he must have been high. Wesley pouted his lips. I did like those lips

"Do it for me?" he whined.

I really liked those lips...

"Fine!" I relented. "But, only for a minute." I took off my clothes and stood in the night, naked save for a pair of briefs. The wind brushed my chest and two chest hairs. I covered my nipples with my arms and the hair on my arms stood on end. It was an unusually cold night for Arkansas

"Are you sure it's not cold? I'm pretty sure it's cold." I asked

"It's practically steaming!" Wesley smiled

I couldn't believe I was doing this, I was *not* the kind of guy to do things like this. I was more the kind of guy who keeps his shirt on at swimming pools. I wasn't outgoing, I didn't like to make a big scene or draw attention to myself. I was far more comfortable blending in with the background. It was Wesley who was the adventurous one. He would always take over whatever room he was in, give him five minutes and he'd be the center of attention. He was the class clown, always making jokes and snide remarks, and getting in trouble with the teachers. I've had to meet him after detention many times.

I've known Wesley most of my life. We've been best friends since pre-k. I knew Wesley was gay since eighth grade, when he made a big deal of making sure everyone knew. We didn't become a couple until about a year ago when I finally came out to him. I wasn't like Wesley, I wasn't confident in who I was and I didn't want anyone to know. I still hadn't told anyone else.

"Come on!" Wesley prodded. I stepped into the water and the cold shot up my legs. It felt like stepping into a pile of knives, well I think I've never done that before, but it feels like it should be the same

"You lied!" I laughed. "It's freezing!"

"No it's not! Don't be a baby. Come closer." I stepped deeper into the water and it went up my thigh and reached my groin. I felt my balls hit my heart and let out a yelp.

"Fuck that's cold!" I screamed. Wesley started to laugh. I stepped closer and the water reached my stomach. I winced but eventually made my way to him. He wrapped his arms around me and pulled me closer.

"See? That wasn't so bad." We stared at each other and Wesley suddenly fell backwards and we splashed into the water. The cold was intense at first, but soon my body grew used to it.

After a moment Wesley brought us up. I gasped for air.

"What the hell, Wes!" I yelled, wiping the water from my eyes.

"I'm sorry, I couldn't resist!" Wesley laughed. "You should see the look on your face, it's kind of cute." He kissed me and I kissed back. It was a perfect moment and I didn't want it to end. We pulled away and looked into each other's eyes. Wesley was so handsome. His smile was this goofy lopsided grin and he had this one tooth that went crooked. I stared at his face, taking in every curve and freckle, every pore.

"Love you." I whispered. And I did, It was the first time I said it to him. I had felt this way for a while, but was afraid of scaring him. But in that moment I felt something, something real, something good. I wish I still did.

Wesley stayed silent, staring into my eyes. I anxiously watched his lip, waiting for him to say it back or smile or do anything. He splashed my face with water and burst out laughing. I laughed too, hiding my disappointment.

"I'm gonna kill you!" I splashed back. We messed around in the water for an hour, splashing and swimming. Eventually, we grew tired and headed for the car. Water dripped from our bodies and the air pierced our wet skin.

We stood against the car drip drying. I crossed my arms and shivered so Wesley put his arm around me and pulled my body to his. The two of us stood together and shared body heat. I had never felt closer to another. To be exposed like this together. To be fighting the cold, relying on one another for warmth. It made me feel as though we were the same person. Our skin touched and I felt as if there was no difference between my body and his. I grabbed hold of Wesley's face, pulled it to mine, and looked into his eyes.

"I love you." I pulled him closer and kissed him. We held onto each other not wanting to pull away. Wesley's kiss grew more aggressive and he held me tighter. His hand began to move down from my back to my hips. I grew tense, Wesley didn't notice. This was it, I thought, our first time. I grew increasingly nervous. His hands moved to my waistband and my whole body tensed up. Wesley pulled my underwear down and I jolted back, now fully exposed.

"What's wrong?" He asked, reaching for me. I receded further at his gesture. What was wrong? I had been waiting for this moment for a long time, fantasizing about how romantic it'd be. I pictured us looking into each other's eyes and sharing a moment, but this just felt crude.

"I just don't think I'm feeling it right now." I pulled up my briefs and hugged my chest. He laughed.

"It looks like you're feeling it." Wesley motioned toward my groin, where I now had a hard on.

I grabbed my clothes and tried to dress.

"I'm just not feeling it." I said. Wesley snatched my clothes from my hands and threw them down.

"What's the matter? Is it because we're outside? No one's gonna see us." He put his hand on my chest and I felt all my atoms trying to back away. "It'll be fun, you'll like it" He smiled. "I thought you loved me."

"I do Wes, but I just don't want to right now. I'm tired and we need to get home." I hoped he'd accept the excuse but he just continued to stroke my chest.

"Don't you think we've waited long enough? We've been together a year and you've barely let me do anything."

"Wesley, I said no." I was feeling really uncomfortable and just wanted to get dressed and drive home. But Wesley wasn't giving in.

"Come on Danny, I think you're hot and you *Obviously* think I am too." His cold hands sent chills through my bones. "Besides, seeing you in that underwear has gotten me all excited. You don't want to leave me hanging right?"

"If you're so horny go behind that tree and take care of business, I won't judge" I joked, trying to ease the tension. Wesley didn't seem amused.

"I can't keep waiting for you to grow up Daniel. You're my boyfriend and this is what boyfriends do." He stared into my eyes and they shown with a bit of anger. I wish he'd let it go but he just kept staring. Maybe it would be easier if I just let him do it. I let out a sigh.

"Fine, but just this once." Wesley didn't say anything, he just took off his boxers and started kissing me. This time the kiss wasn't romantic, it was just rough and forceful. Eventually we ended up on the ground and Wesley ended up inside me. It was a weird feeling that I didn't enjoy. Once again our bodies seemed to combine but this time it didn't feel like we were becoming one, it felt like he was consuming me, making me his. As Wesley kept thrusting towards me, he made grunts and guttural noises that made him seem like an animal, and me feel like his prey. I wanted it to stop, I tried to speak up but I couldn't seem to get the words out. Instead all I could do was release a single strangled groan and he seemed to think this meant I was enjoying it.

"See I told you." He said as he continued to push himself deeper into my body. I could feel him inside me, hurting me. Soon I gave in and tried to think of something else until it was over. When he finished he fell away from me and laid on his back. I turned on my side to look away from him. "Wasn't that fun?" He asked "Aren't you glad we finally did it?"

"Sure" I answered "now can we go home?"

"Fine," He said. We stood and put our clothes on. Even though I was clothed I still felt exposed. "I love you too," he said and quickly kissed my cheek. We walked to the car.

Over the next couple weeks I continued to let Wesley have sex with me, and each time I hated it more and more. I began to feel sick whenever Wesley wanted to hang out, I knew what he wanted to do. I'd get so nervous that I'd throw up. I started having trouble sleeping and would just lay awake for hours. The worst part was that I didn't know why I hated it so much. Isn't this what every teenage boy is supposed to want? Aren't we supposed to go crazy over sex? Was I broken?

To be honest I've never really cared about sex, I've never even seen porn. I jerked off but it was more for the feeling, it was never about someone else. I never really had crushes before Wesley. All the other boys would talk about the girls they liked and I just sat silently, pretending to relate. I always thought this was because I'm gay, but now I'm not so sure. Why do I hate it?

Maybe there's just something wrong with me.

I tried watching porn, just to see if I could enjoy it. I tried gay porn, straight porn, I tried all kinds, even crazy stuff that made me a little nauseous. But nothing worked. So I kept letting Wesley inside me, hoping that if I just tried to calm down I would enjoy it. I never did.

I kept trying to figure out these feelings, trying to put them into words but none came up. Was I sick? What was the matter with me? That question never left my head, all day and all night. What's the matter with me? Until one day it hit me. Maybe there wasn't anything wrong with me. Maybe this is just how I am. Everybody's different right? Maybe this was just the way I was different. Maybe I didn't need sex to love someone. I loved Wesley long before all this.

Things started to make sense. I had never thought about sex, even when I was waiting to have sex with Wesely it was more about the romance than the actual sex. I was a sucker for romance. I loved all of those old rom coms where the guy always gets the girl and divorce doesn't exist. That's why I loved Wesley, it wasn't about wanting to have sex with him, it was just about wanting to *be* with him. I felt like I had finally found the answer I didn't even know I was looking for. It's like that feeling you get when you finally figure out the word you had on the tip of your tongue, like all had been revealed. Like the puzzle pieces finally fit.

I started to get excited. Maybe I could tell Wes and he'd understand. Then we could be happy together again. Then my heart dropped, what if he doesn't understand? What if he doesn't want to be with someone he can't have sex with?

It took me about a month to figure out what to do. During that month I pretended I had a stomach bug so Wesely wouldn't come over. But eventually I decided to tell him. I knew he loved me and thought he would still love me after. If he didn't, then I didn't need him. So I called him and told him I was feeling better. I asked him if he wanted to drive to Little Rock again this weekend. He said yes and so we did.

I sat nervously in his car as we drove. I stared out the

window watching as trees and the occasional car shot past. I wondered who sat in those cars. What other lives were being lived out in those cars? I wondered if there were any other boys struggling to say what I wanted to say. Any other boys trying to find the answers I so desperately was searching for. Any other boys about to be hurt the way I was about to be hurt. My heart was beating a mile a minute and my hands felt slippery with sweat. I glanced over at Wesley. He was softly bobbing his head to a Bob Dylan song. His hair flew back and forth, covering and uncovering his eyes. For a moment I wondered if that was the best thing to do while driving. *Don't get distracted,* I thought, *you need to tell him.*

I let out a shaky sigh and turned off the radio.

"Turn it back on, I like that song." My throat felt dry and I considered dropping it, maybe now wasn't the best time. No, I had to do it. I couldn't keep going on like this.

"I have something to tell you."

"What is it?" He asked. I took a deep breath.

"I don't want to have sex anymore." Wesely slammed on the breaks. For a moment I thought this was how it ended but luckily we were alone on the road. "Jesus, Wes!"

"Are you breaking up with me?"

"No! God, no Wes. I just don't want to have sex anymore." He stared at me for a moment, then he chuckled and started to drive.

"Nice one," he said, "very funny, Danny."

"I'm not joking, Wesley."

"So what are you saying Danny?"

"I'm saying I don't want to have sex with you anymore." I said, glueing my eyes to the road ahead. "I've been thinking about this for a while now."

"What, are you bored?" He asks. "Do we need to try something new?"

"No, Wes. I'm saying I don't want to try anything."

"Is it me?" his face reddens. "Am I not good?"

"No! Well...I don't know." Wesley seemed confused. Oh God, he doesn't understand. How can I make him understand when I don't fully understand myself? I can't seem to find the words. "It's not about you, It's about me." Did I really just say that?

"So you *are* breaking up with me!"

"No, Wesely! I didn't mean for it to sound that way, just listen to me!" He was silent. "I love you, Wes, I just don't want to sleep with you. I mean I don't want to sleep with anyone."

"Danny, you're not making any sense. What the hell are you talking about?"

"I don't think I like sex."

"You don't think?"

"I *know* I don't like sex." Wesley lets out another chuckle and shakes his head.

"Danny, you're confused." There were the words, I always knew I'd hear those words. I just thought it would be from my parents after telling them I'm gay. I didn't think it would come from the boy I loved.

"I'm not confused, Wes. I guess I've felt this way for a while, I just didn't know until now."

"So you don't wanna fuck anymore?" He asked.

"Yeah."

"So what the hell would we do?"

"I don't know...Just hang out, spend time together, like we used to."

"That sounds like a friend Daniel. I don't want to be your friend, I want to be your *boy* friend."

"And you still can be. We can go back to the way things were. Just love each other, without the sex." Wesley pulled the car to the side of the road.

"Are you sure you're over that bug? You're acting stupid right now." This time my face got red. I was filled with anger, sadness, and an overwhelming urge to leave the car. But I pushed that feeling down and stayed. Why couldn't he understand this?

"I'm not acting stupid! I told you I don't like sex!" I yelled.

"You don't know what you like!" Wesely yelled back. Then his voice softened. "You probably just don't like what we're doing and overreacting. You do tend to overreact Danny." He grabbed my hand and held it hard enough that I couldn't pull it back. His fingernails dug into my flesh. "Let's try something new, You'll like it I promise." I tried to pull my hand away again.

"No, Wes, I'm saying no." My heart started pounding. He wouldn't let go of my hand. I need to get out of this car.

"Stop being stupid, Danny." He put his other hand on my thigh. "Trust me, you'll like this." I wanted out, I had to get out.

"Please." I whimper. I move his hand from my thigh but he just puts it back, harder this time. "I don't want to."

"You don't know what you want, I'll help you." Wesley crossed over to my seat and got on top of me. He put his lips on mine. I groaned and tried to move away but he just held my neck with his hand. "Just let me do this."

I started to pound on his back but he forced my hands down. He put all of his weight on me and I felt crushed underneath. I could barely breathe. I felt so powerless. I just wanted out of the car. I tried to do something, anything but I couldn't move. I tried to scream but he covered my mouth. "Don't fight me. I promise you'll enjoy this." Then he started. "You like that don't you?"

I just wanted out of the car.

I wanted to fight, I wanted to push him away and beat him senseless. I wanted to bash in his face and just keep hitting. Until he was gone. But he was so heavy and I couldn't find the strength to keep fighting. He was so heavy and it felt like lifting a mountain. Soon I just gave in, I stopped fighting and just tried to climb into myself. Tried to ignore what was going on, pretend I didn't notice what was being taken from me. I tried to make it all disappear, maybe if I just closed my eyes tight enough it would all go away.

I heard a car approaching, it didn't stop.

"Doesn't this feel good?"

I just wanted out.

I can't remember what happened next. I just remember walking home. Walking through the Arkansas countryside. My shoes were gone. I don't remember when I lost them. My pants were ripped and I was no longer wearing underwear. Blood dripped down my thigh. I looked up at the stars in the sky and suddenly felt so small, so useless. weak. I started to cry.

I ended up back home and took a bath. I turned the water as high as it could go and sat in the scorching heat. I wanted to burn the night away, maybe if I just burned it away I wouldn't have to think about it again. I felt sick, how could he do this to me? I thought he loved me, I thought I loved him. I didn't know what to do, where to go. I didn't want to think about it, but the thoughts wouldn't stop. I slid down and laid in the water. I can't stop seeing it, smelling it, tasting it. I just wanted it to stop. I slid my head under the water and the world became muffled. I just wanted to not think. I didn't bring my head back up.

I woke up in the hospital. I didn't know how long I had been there. My parents were there and they started crying when they saw I was awake. A doctor came by later and told me I showed signs of being raped. My mom let out a cry and my dad wouldn't look at me. The doctor told me I was lucky to be found when I was and that I should be ok in a few days. When he left the room my mom wrapped her arms around me, still crying. My dad just looked out the window, his shoulders shaking up and down. Then Wesley entered the room and the air chilled.

"You're awake." He says.

"I am." Acid filled my throat and I couldn't look him in the eyes.

"I was worried, I told your parents about us."

"You did?"

"Yeah, how we've been dating and how you were afraid to tell them." My mother squeezes me tighter.

"We don't care, baby, We're just happy you're ok."

I wasn't.

A pair of police officers walked into the room.

"Daniel O'Reilly? We just have a couple of questions." The first officer said in a soft tone.

"Ok."

"Do you remember what happened last night?"

"We were heading to the city for the weekend." Wesley

answered. “We got in a fight and Danny got upset and went to walk home. I tried to stop him, he must have gotten jumped on the way home.” Bullshit.

“What were you fighting about?”

“Danny wanted to have sex for the first time, he had planned this whole weekened. I told him I wasn’t ready and he got upset.” Total bullshit.

The second officer turned to me. “Is this true son?” Wesley shot me a look and I wanted to melt into the bed.

“Yes, that’s right.” I answered.

“Do you remember who did this to you?” the first officer asked. I glanced at Wesley and he was staring straight at me, his fists clenched. I felt like I was back in the car.

“No, I don’t” My eyes fell. The police asked a few more questions and then left. The second officer turned back and looked at me like I was a lost puppy. Then they were gone. After a few days I was released and went home.

They put me on some depression meds and referred me to a therapist. I put off seeing her for months, I thought I could handle it. She told me that there were others like me, people who didn’t want sex. That there was a word for it, Asexuality. A community. I wasn’t alone, I wasn’t broken. I even met a boy, his name is Matt, he’s not asexual but he doesn’t mind if we don’t have sex. He’s happy to have me for who I am. I’m not sure I love him, not sure I’m ready for that again, but maybe someday. It isn’t all sunshine and rainbows though. I still have trouble in cars and I don’t like being touched. It took me a while to accept what he did to me.

He raped me. That’s the first time I’ve said it. He raped me. And not just that one time, but all the other times too. Times when he must have seen I was uncomfortable but didn’t care. He betrayed me. I loved him, *loved.* I’m not sure how to move through this but I want to try. I want help. I know now that he didn’t love me and that I deserve better. I know who I am now and that I’m not broken, even if he tried to break me. I’m not ok, but I think I will be.

A few days ago I got a call from Wesley.

"Danny? I'm really sorry man, I didn't mean to hurt you, I just got mixed signals. Can you forgive me?" I let the words hang in the air. I let them float away and disappear. I stood silent with the phone to my ear. "Danny?" I hung up the phone and blocked his number.

Heart Shaped Bruises

Cassi Dillon

CW: Abuse

Callus hands
On a body
That you claimed
For no reason
Other than
Greed

I don't remember
What belonging to myself
Feels like

My soul withered with every touch
Your darkness wrapped itself around me
Like a heavy quilt
Stored in all of my vacant spaces

Wandering hands
Never waiting for a green light

Rushed movements
Trying to get what you wanted
Before I can mumble out a
No

Your hands left bruises
On places
They never
Should
Have
Been

red nailpolish

Mia Lehmkuhl

red.

i was only 5 years old
when you told me
red nailpolish was for hookers.

the worst of the worst
the whores and women of the night
all unified
by one single color

growing up
red turned into one of many favorite colors
i admired the color of blood
and of love

the way red rushes through veins
and pumps through our hearts
it can be the greatest tragedy
and your loveliest romance

but then again
red was for hookers
so i cast aside my beating heart
and let my veins run dry

i rejected red
like cold feet at the altar
i painted my nails white
to please you

white was all i knew
for a time
with my legs crossed and my head down
i too said, red was for hookers.

then, something caught my eye
i began to notice
that the only woman i saw in red

was you.

Primal

Olivia Williams

when I was young everyone said how much
I looked like You / now that I am grown they say I look like
mom /
I don't know if they think that because I actually do or if
because they *think*
I'm a — [woman]
it's Our personality that is similar / Our eyes / Our laugh
it's genetics / DNA /
is it how We share the primal urge to find a woman?
to love / to touch / consume / absorb /
the way We mirror a bear —
use the edge of a doorway to scratch Your back / I learned to
copy you

(the moment I realized how much I was
like you) like the bear in the tall
redwood / forest

climbing, hunting, foraging, scratching, sleeping
/ it's in Our blood /
I rely on my senses / I used to mirror what you do

through this evolution I have surpassed both who You are
and used to be
I am the new species / even Darwin couldn't have predicted
\ 'discovered' /
devote Your life and believe in a religion that has cursed me
/ for following my instincts
I know what it is to be one with nature — *I am natural* / it's
primal
the way it is for You
that is how it feels for Me

The World

Cambel Castle

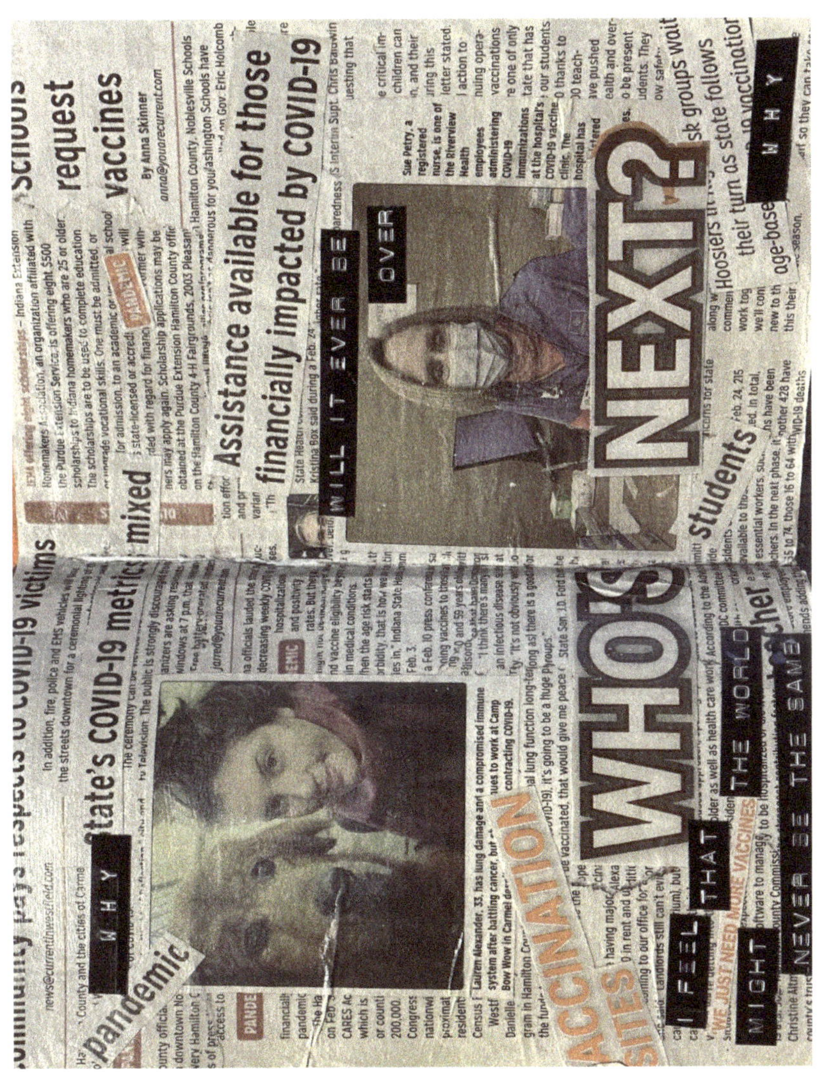

Mixed Media

This piece was created to express some feelings about COVID-19 and a way to document the experience.

Let Me Cry

Brooklyn Harpold et. al

CW: Sexual Assault

Composer: Brooklyn Harpold
Lyricist: Emma Knaack
Performers: Elizabeth Enderle and Lauren Neilson

In this piece, the speaker plays the role of a victim of sexual assault while the violin plays the role of our society which tries to silence women who speak out about their trauma. Multiple times throughout the piece you may notice the violin interrupting the speaker to emphasize this point. I hope that this composition allows others to see how important it is that we support women that are brave enough to speak up about sexual assault and be a voice for those that can't.

Masculine Androgyny

Zoe Wilkinson

I want to be feminine
in the way that boys are

I want to be masculine
in the way that girls are

I don't like my chest
but I don't *mind* my breasts

When I wear men's T-shirts
just knowing the sleeves aren't capped
affords me a boost of euphoria

I look at men in their 20's
with fluffy short hair

And I point and yell "gender"
because I envy them

I refuse to use purses
because that means I'm a "woman"
(and they're uncomfortable)

I'm scared of the side effects
of HRT pestering my tactile sensitivity
(and I sweat enough as it is)

I want to look queer-coded
like a cartoon villain
and I want to be told

by some old miserable man
that I look like a slut

that cops would beat in the 50's

I want him to misgender me
to soak in his frustration
as he fails miserably

He'll call me a girl
and I'll tell him he's wrong
He'll call me a boy

and he'll be wrong again
he'll resort to "freak"
and I'll thank him for the neopronouns

And I want an ally
who can't define "nonbinary"
to ask what my pronouns are

Simply because
they can't judge me by eye

Ambiguity

Sabrina Camargo

Me dicen güerita
No morenita
Quien soy?

Where are you from
Who me—Or my parents
Depends who asks

Why can't I just be *me*

Hablas muy bonito el español a pesar de haber nacido aquí
Y el novio
Le deberias de ayudar a tus papás

The brown girl with good grades
The brown girl with only white friends
Who am I?

You're really pale for a Mexican, look I'm tanner than her
You don't have an accent when you speak English
You're actually smart, are you sure Spanish is your first language

Why can't I just be *me*

Too Mexicana to be American
Too American to be Mexicana
What am I?

I walk with my head high in search to accept *me*

The Spanish Doll

Karen Newman

When I was a child, I acquired a Spanish doll, a flamenco dancer with delicate, plastic arms and a long, lacy red and white dress with a tight bodice and crinoline train that flowed behind her in a sweeping arc. Her hair was dark, a bit like mine, and tied up in an artful bun with a faux turtle-shell comb holding it in place, and her flashy eye makeup and bright lipstick smile contrasted strongly with her creamy skin tone. She wore black plastic high-heeled shoes, one of which managed to get lost, despite the care I lavished upon her and all my other dolls. Her arms and castanet-bearing fingers were frozen in front of her in a dancer's pose, but much to my consternation, the cat ate off her splayed pinky and index fingers soon after I positioned her on my bedroom dresser. She had an odd allure for me—part ingenue and part vamp, artifact of a culture and language that I didn't know—representing an idealized standard of beauty and a dance that I'd never actually seen performed.

This type of doll was a common Spanish souvenir of the day and came in different sizes. I can't recall now if I selected her myself from a store or if she was given to me by someone who'd just returned from a trip to Spain. Many of my female classmates also displayed identical Spanish dolls in their bedrooms, only theirs had pink or yellow lacy dresses. Her dress couldn't be removed, as she was really meant to be admired in a china cabinet and not actually played with—which was, admittedly, a bit frustrating for the 7-year-old me who delighted in dressing my dolls for various imagined occasions.

She is now lost to the ebb and flow of time that filters through my mind's eye and to the three household moves we made during my childhood. I loved that doll for the mysterious femininity she represented, while simultaneously resenting her impractical extravagance and frippery. Perhaps she was in one of the boxes that went mysteriously missing when we moved to California, along with my girl scout uniform and sash festooned with badges, or perhaps she is at the bottom of a still-unopened box in my parents' garage, decades after the move, her dress inhabited by the silverfish that I will someday encounter when I clean out their house.

S.A.M.

Riley Childers

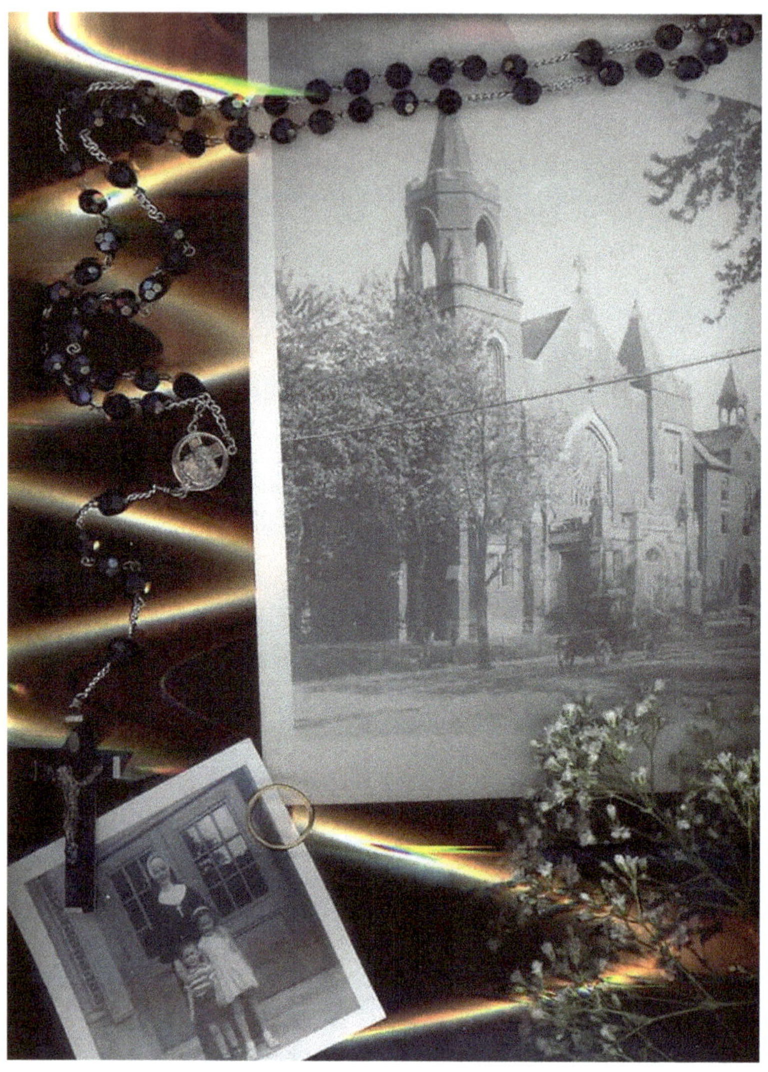

Photograph

"S.A.M." was an experimental photo with practicing scanography. This allows me to bring old photos and create something new and interesting.

Catharsis

Grace Carrender

Trapped in my cranial abyss
Engulfed by putrid skies

Chained lungs
Staunched breaths

Thoughts like stale bubble gum
    the sweetness of life all drained away

Chicken wire holds back the floodgates
I remain encased in a clay jar of my own making

Broken thoughts
Broken brain

Relapse is temporary right?
    God I pray.

    Healing is not the absolution of suffering

    We learn to care for the demons inside
            coaxing them into coexistence

The steel once wired into my mandible unhinges

The golden rays ease the months of pain
    the pain of no one understanding
    the pain of allowing myself to believe no one understands

The Call

Trey Nobbe

Buzz, Buzz, Buzz
Shaking like a dancer
He picks it up, as one does
Silence—my best friend cries—cancer

The months of sickness,
The nights, so sleepless
My feeble friend falling fast
Any day—could be his last

Buzz, Buzz, Buzz—the cell phone wails
Shaking like a dancer,
Like an assassin it never fails—
It steals my friend, f*** you cancer

Fly on the Wall

Olivia Williams

the only times i've seen my father cry have been
at funerals,
    church,
        and the day he came home from the emergency room.
he walked in
        still dressed for work

(i look back and wonder how long he sat in his new car waiting for the courage to come into this place we call home)

once he passed my room and saw my mother in the kitchen
                                        well....
it was over.

CANCER.

<u>**5 spots**</u> spread within him.
                [spleen, kidney, lungs, spine, and colon]

he choked, sputtered, and gasped for air.

he shook and was paler than i'd ever seen him.

            my mother walked him to their room. i followed.
a fly on the wall...
i listened
i looked from him to her

she cried and was already in denial   *this can't be real. holy shit. what are we going to do?*

it is strange to be the faithless one between the three in the
        room
we cry
        we choke
they pray
        we take it one step each day.

While My Father Dies

Christopher Schmidt

"He's going to a better place," they lie
whenever I see them.
But I get it; it's easier isn't it?
They have kids, families,
mortgages, schedules.
We all do. But how will I even step
toward the door after that barrage of kisses
he's given? How do I say, "I've seen
you enough today?"
I shuffle to my car, where I sit
paralyzed, like a poet or painter,
who is rapt by all the wretchedness of life—
its odors and dampness.

In the morning my father rests in
bed like Ahkenaten: 145 pounds
and counting, down another 10 this week.
Will more flesh resign from its duties and melt into
his sheets with his sweat and pee? Then what?
And what do I hope for: more time for him to skeletonize,
to forget what day it is, to have more strangers
scurry off with his modesty?
Does it matter? Where does my hope fit in anyway?
He hopes to go home in a few weeks;
his protruding pelvis and sunken chest
apparently are not sufficiently off-putting to him.
And, wow, he almost stood yesterday! Is this
when we, his sons, gallop in with heroic cries
of "rage, rage against the dying of the light"?
Or, should my brothers and I plan for the day
we fold his arms across his chest, and dress
him for his tomb?
On that day, in-laws and neighbors will speak

of the joy that his suffering has ended.
No doubt, the funeral chatter will be of the serenity ahead,
because it pacifies the chatterers so.
And, finally, lives will resume, no longer interrupted by the
inconvenience of phone calls about another fall down the
        stairs.
Until then, I'll continue to praise his grip and his smile. I'll
encourage him to use his legs to build their strength. I'll
congratulate him for eating all his food and
drinking all his water. I'll remind him how much he is cared for
in this place no one wants to be,
and that he is doing well and making good progress.
At the end of this day, I'll get my kisses, and give my hugs.
Over and over I'll ask if he needs anything
and it will take me too long to leave.
Because I hate closing his door behind me;
and because I know I am a liar too.

Fog City Solstice

Dean Wiseman

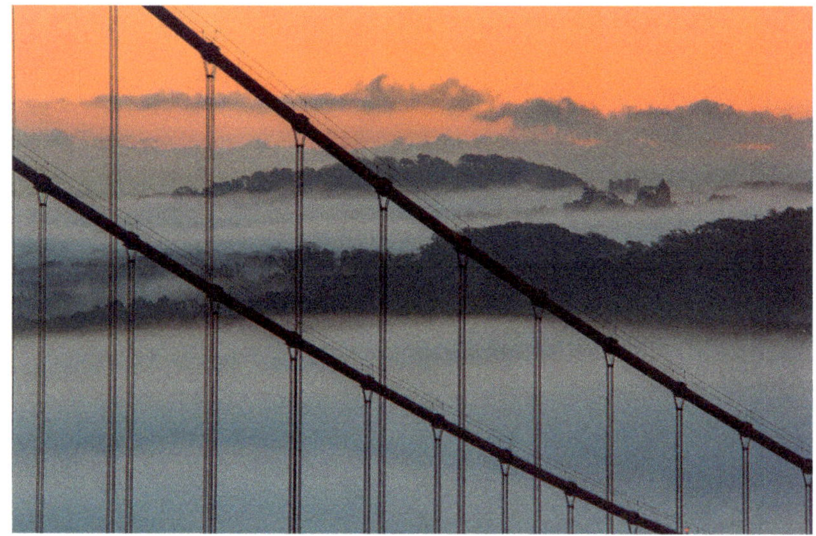

Photograph

I have had the good fortune of being able to visit San Francisco more than any other major city outside the midwest. It didn't hurt that I have a career in biomedical research, as major research conferences are held there on a frequent basis. However, almost all of those visits happen in either in

Golden Gate Winter Solstice

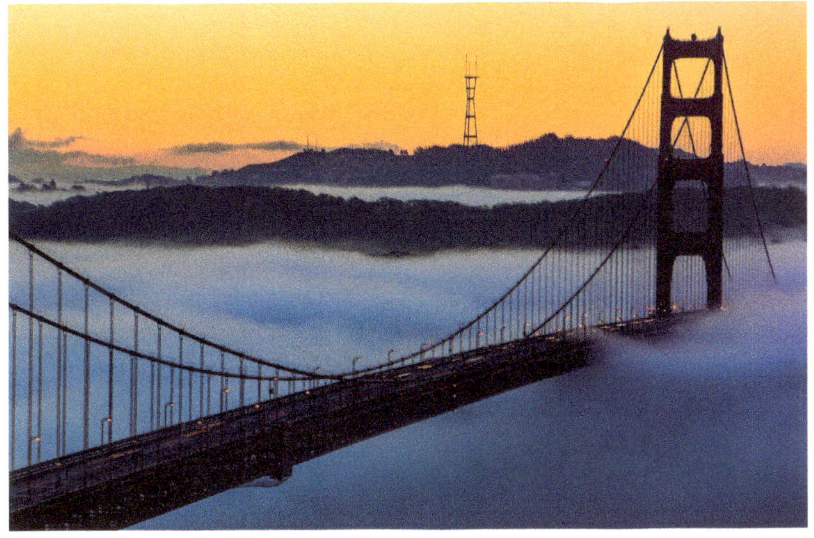

Photograph

the spring or summer—rarely if ever in the winter time. The combination of the low winter solstice sun and the fog one evening around sunset on Treasure Island just east of the city, or sunrise a day later at Golden Gate, was a surreal experience. Both times, I encountered some local photography enthusiasts

Bay City Solstice

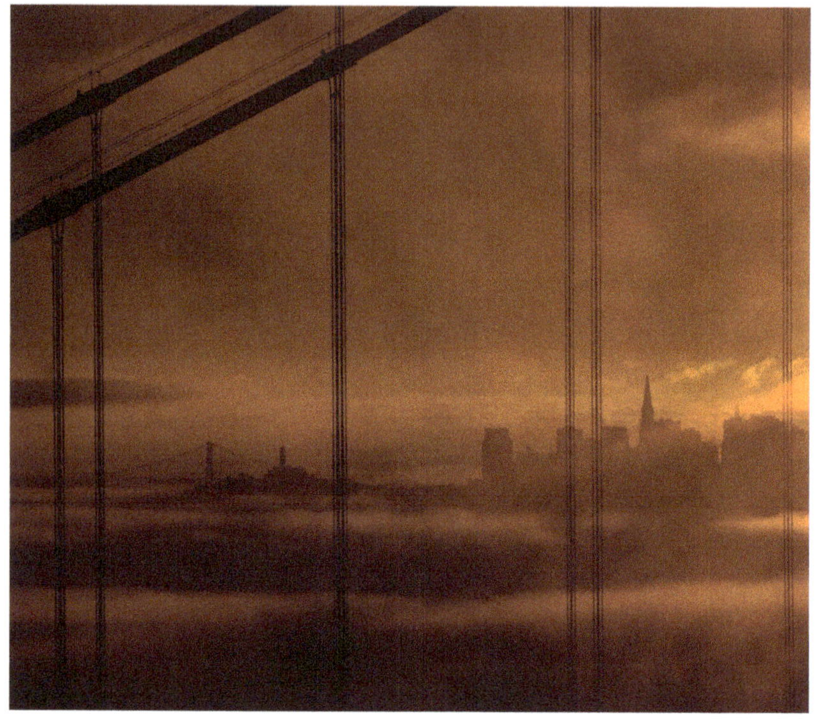

Photograph

shooting in the area, and I took it as a very good sign seeing them get excited! I only hope that I can get back to take more photos...It's no understatement to say the Bay Area and San Francisco is a photographer's dream!

Living, Loving and Surviving in a Post Apocalyptic America

CariAnn Freed

March.
In my small apartment on
the southside of the city
I woke up to the apocalypse.
Death to life before You
and Death to life after.

April.
Waking up to love is
almost better than falling
asleep in it. I hope they
never find us.

May.
Who are You if not magic,
if not lightening–
I'll follow You into every
tomorrow.

June.
My world split like
tectonic plates,
A Black lava came
bubbling between them
like violent, like war–
 Like too dark to make nice

Too violent to live within
the Earth,
Too fluid to be captured
Too angry for sorry
Through clouds of smoke
and red flash I saw you

smiling,
I heard your laugh,
But post apocalyptic America is nasty,
Busted up and bleeding
black blood all over
When I look at me I see
my mother's arms all the
way to my hands,
Her nose, plus my
grandma's cheeks.

After the explosion of June
I'm here shaking in **July,**

There's a pile of dishes in
the sink,
When I pass through the
kitchen I can hear my
father say,
"Just get it done,"

But I'll go back to bed and
stare at the closet where
A powder pink dress hangs
from a wedding I never
made it to,

My first friend, she taught me
how to laugh
She never let me think I
wasn't cool,

Now the sound of her
giggle burns slow between
the bubbles and the black,
I think I'm saving the
powder pink fabric
just in case another war

breaks out,
I'll use it as a dressing in
case we ever get caught in
the crossfire

August.
In post apocalyptic
America I found love
and loss.
Now we wake up everyday
and choose each other.

Even if it's different now,
Even if it hurts,
Even when it bleeds.

I choose You because we
have hopes and dreams
that are bigger than
diamonds
Bigger than disaster,
Bigger than Truth

Bigger than my small
apartment on the southside

I fell in love underneath all
the city,
Beneath the brimstone,
and the asphalt,
Beneath the darkness and
into the self

At the heart of the center,
the deepest of depths

The black and the bubble.

Sometimes We Die a Few Times and That's Alright

Mackenzie Hyatt

I haven't died before
unless you count the times I've wanted to
and then, theoretically,
there exist alternate versions of me,
who, like moles, live
blind, confined to earth.

A man on a bus told everyone
that he'd died six times,
two-thirds of a cat,
all on one ambulance ride.
Legally dead,
like there's a license for it.

I wanted to ask if he'd seen a god there
or if he even got past Processing,
if there's a chatty secretary
and if she's pretty. I wanted to ask him,
on his next trip,
if he could check if it's too late for me to change my mind.

Sometimes I wonder if what I'm doing is right.
If poking at shattered skulls is morally justifiable.
Then I wonder if the skull
could be my ancient cousin.
Will I strike a kinsman with my trowel blade?

A part of me,
some twisted, wishful part of me,
hopes that I get buried carefully enough
and that all of our records are lost enough
that my skull or a single rib
will be an exciting find to some future me

and I'll get free museum admission for life.

The Long View

Mary Redman

A squalling red-faced infant
knows life for what it is
sudden intrusion
of warm-cold, dark-light,
wet-dry, quiet-loud.
At first breath, a gasp, a cry
she knows the concurrence
of opposites.
Clear voices speaking in tongues,
slippery hands pulling
gentle arms pressing
head to breast,
a sigh,
it has begun: asleep-awake.

A rattling grey-faced ancient
knows life for what it is
sudden intrusion
of warm-cold, light-dark,
dry-wet, loud-quiet.
At last breath, a gasp, a cry
she knows the concurrence
of opposites.
Clear voices speaking in tongues,
familiar faces out of focus
tear-smeared smiles
lips to hands,
a sigh,
it has ended: awake-asleep.

2020 Whirling Prize Winners

Poetry Winner: *Red Mother* by Laurel Radzieski

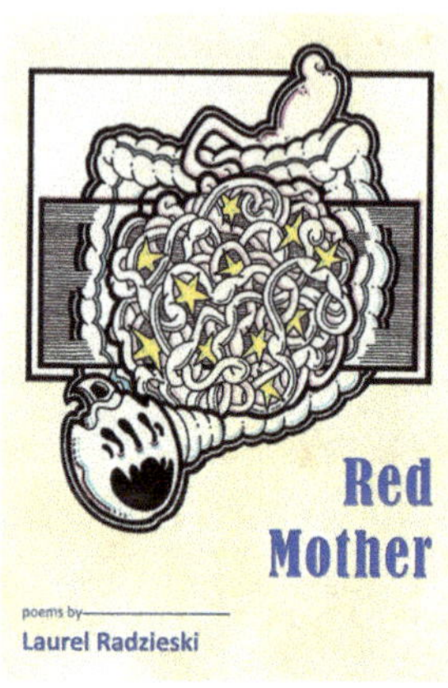

In *Red Mother*, Laurel Radzieski weaves a love story told from the perspective of a parasite. This series of short poems explores the intimacy, desire and devotion we all experience by following the sometimes tender, often distressing relationship that emerges between a parasite and its host. Radzieski's poetry is playful, though often with sinister undertones. Far from romanticizing either role, Red Mother takes readers on a tour of their own innards, exposing the hooks and claws of all involved. Following the parasite's life cycle, the book blurs the line between science and poetic license to create a fantastical romp not for the squeamish. Although parasites are not known as conversationalists, Radzieski's guest has a lot to say.

Prose Winner: *The Penguin Book of Exorcisms* edited by Joseph P. Laycock

Believe it or not, fifty-seven percent of Americans believe in demonic possession. Spirit possession has been documented for thousands of years and across religions and cultures, even into our time. *The Penguin Book of Exorcisms*, edited by religious studies scholar Joseph P. Laycock, showcases a range of stories, beliefs, and practices surrounding exorcism from across time, cultures and religions. Laycock's exhaustive research incorporates scientific papers, letters and diary entries by the clergy, treatises by physicians and theologians, reports from missionaries and colonial officers, legal proceedings, and poetry and popular legends. The result is informative and entertaining, and proves that truth can indeed be scarier than fiction.

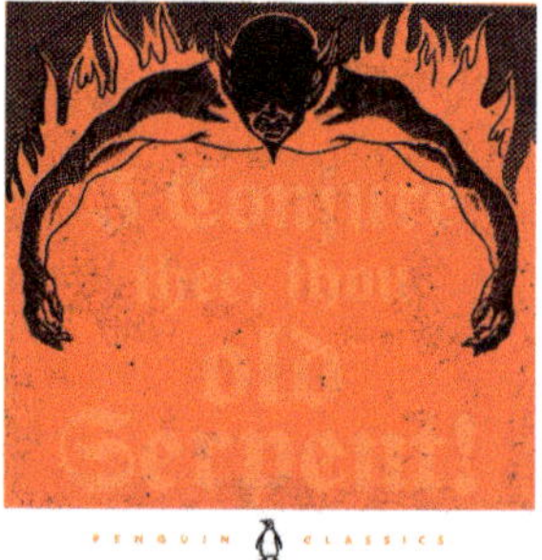

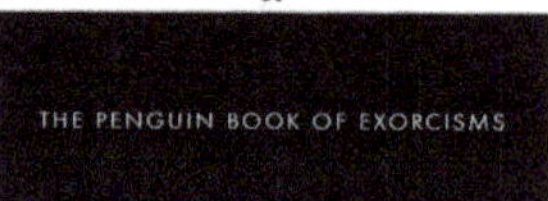

2021 Chapbook in Poetry Winner

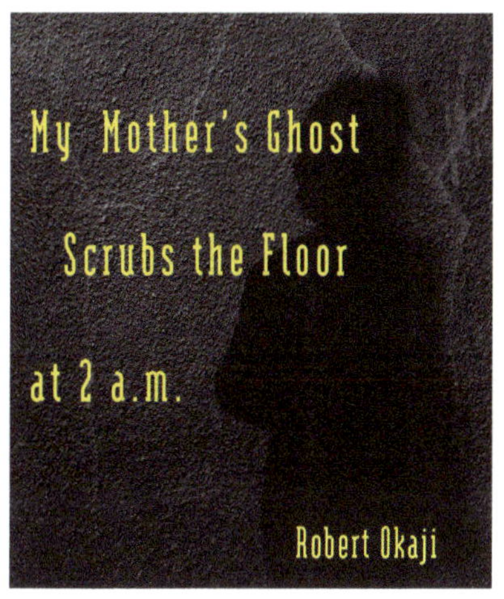

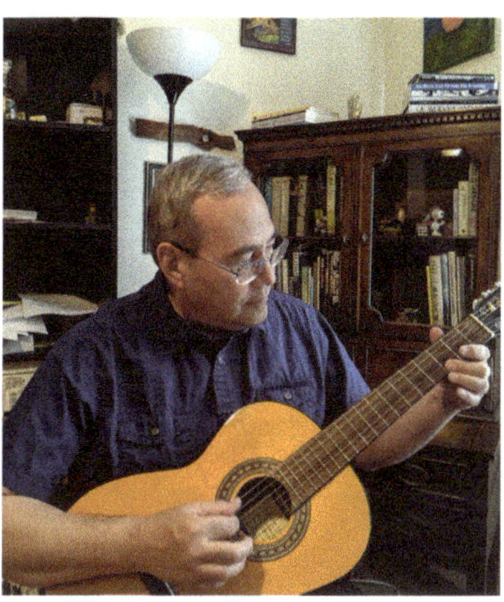

Robert Okaji's chapbook, *My Mother's Ghost Scrubs the Floor at 2 a.m.*, is a beautiful collection of poetry that grapples with the theme of loss. In this book, Okaji uses imagery in his poems to describe his mother and the void she left behind. This gorgeous, heart wrenching collection takes us on a journey of learning how to keep the memories of the people we love close to our hearts and helps us remember that they never truly leave us even after they're gone. Okaji creates a feeling of familiarity that lets anyone who's experienced a loss relate to this book.

Robert Okaji is a displaced Texan living in Indiana. A seven-time Pushcart Prize nominee, he holds a BA in history, served without distinction in the U.S. Navy, lived the hand-to-mouth existence of a bookstore owner, worked as a university administrator, and most recently, bagged groceries for a living. He is the author of multiple chapbooks, and his poetry has appeared or is forthcoming in *Taos Journal of International Poetry & Art, Boston Review, North Dakota Quarterly, Panoply, Vox Populi, Indianapolis Review, Book of Matches, Slippery Elm* and elsewhere. Visit his blog, *O at the Edges*, at robertokaji.com.

2021 Chapbook in Prose Winner

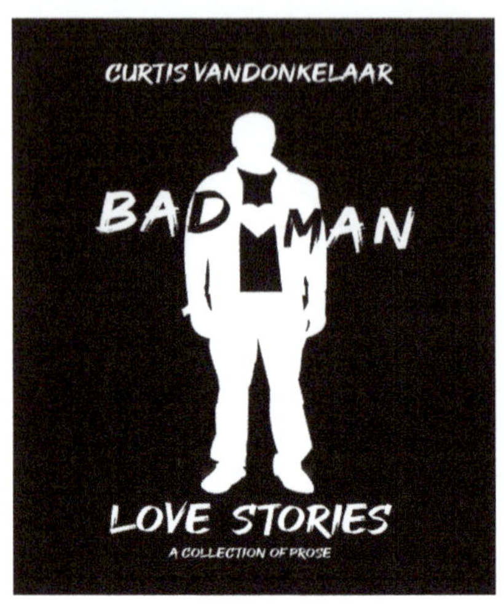

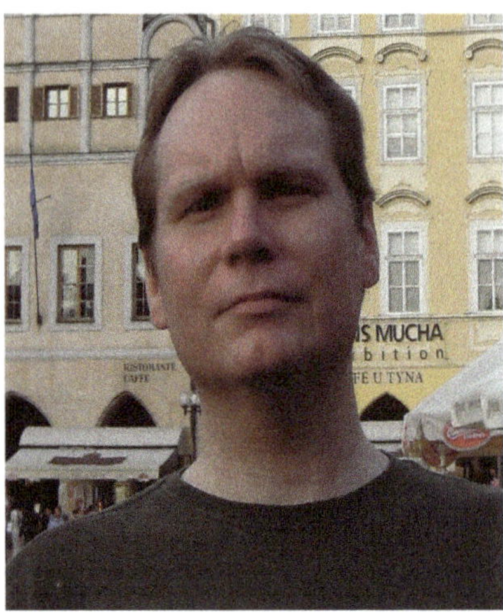

Curtis VanDonKelaar's book of prose, *Bad Man Love Stories*, is a page-turner collection of stories that will keep you hooked. In these stories, VanDonKelaar portrays themes such as guilt, lust, regret, and envy. Each story is about an interesting man and an issue he is struggling with from raising kids, divorces, or accepting a new change in their life. This hilarious, and sometimes heartbreaking collection will take you on a roller coaster of emotions that will keep you reading to the very end.

Curtis Vandonkelaar's work has won prizes in the *Literal Latte* Short Short Contest, the *Gateway Review's* Speculative Flash Fiction Contest, and the Press 53 *Prime Number Magazine* Flash Fiction Contest. His stories have appeared in *Fifth Wednesday, J Journal, Aquifer: The Florida Review Online*, the *Vestal Review*, *Western Humanities Review*, *Hobart*, and *DIAGRAM*, among others, and have been finalists with the *Puerto del Sol* Fiction Contest, *The Laurel Review's* Midwestern Fiction Contest, *Harpur Palate's* John Gardner Fiction Contest, the *Tusculum Review* Fiction Contest, *Pulp Literature's* Hummingbird Prize for Flash Fiction, and *Passages North's* Neutrino Prize. See curtisvandonkelaar.com for writings and more.

2021 Novella Winner

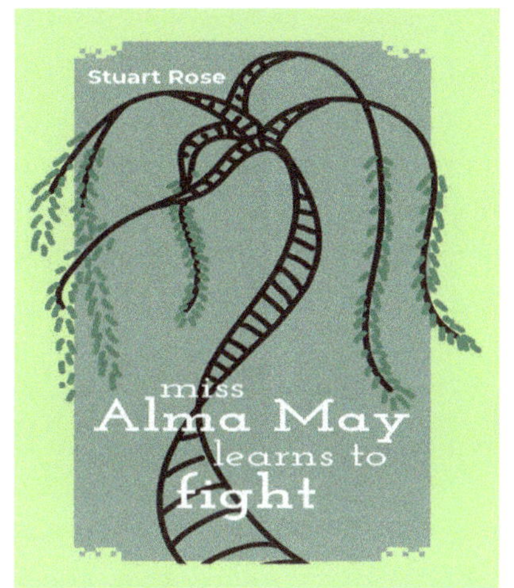

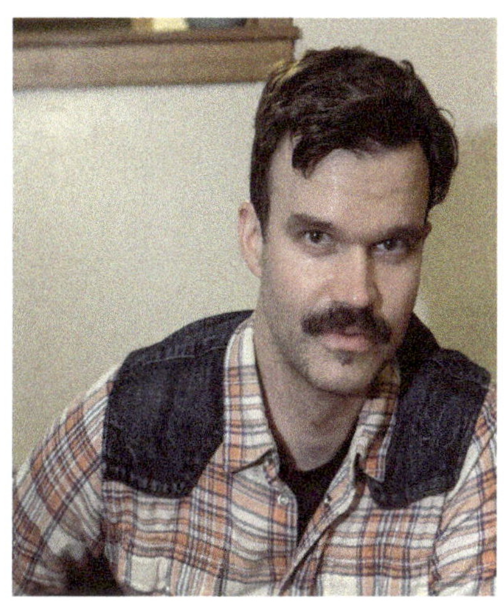

Stuart Rose's novella, *Miss Alma May Learns to Fight*, is an empowering story about learning how to be strong and stand up for yourself. The story follows the character Miss Alma May, a woman who carries a lot of anger inside her, but doesn't know how to stand up to people when faced with confrontation. As she begins learning martial arts and feels more confident and in control of her life she learns to fight back effectively without letting the anger she feels consume her. This wonderful story is a message of strength and perseverance that is well worth the read.

Stuart Rose is an MFA student at the Rainier Writing Workshop at Pacific Lutheran University. He is employed by the U.S. Forest Service as a seasonal trails worker and enjoys playing his guitar so loudly that it wakes up his cat. Stuart lives and works in Montana.

Contributor Biographies

Ali Viewegh is a junior at UIndy majoring in English (literary studies) and secondary education and minoring in creative writing with an honors concentration. Currently, she is the co-Design Editor for *Etchings Volume 34.1*, secretary for SEA, and one of the Assistants to the Writing Lab director. She loves writing and hopes to be able to spread different messages through her writing. Eventually, she would love to have her book published.

Adam Lourenco Fernandes is a lover of music, art, and people. He is a senior visual communication design student with a keen interest in typography and brand identity design. He also has a knack for playing guitar and singing. He was once stuck in an airport with a delayed flight and his guitar. A custodial staff asked Adam to play a song for her. Being stuck in an airport, it seemed fitting to sing "Yesterday" by The Beatles. The custodial told him that he made her day. Adam thought that as long as he was able to do something like that, he'd be happy forever.

Armani Stewart is a senior majoring in English (creative writing) at the University of Indianapolis. Ever since she was a child, she's always had a deep love and value for writing and creativity. When it comes to poetry writing—one of her utmost favorite hobbies—she does her best to incorporate vivid imagery and details in her poetry to make readers feel as if they are there themselves, and, most importantly, each piece of writing she creates is not only deep, but also tells a story. She enjoys giving her readers the opportunity to let their imaginative minds wander and form their own meaning of each poetic story.

Asiah Avery is a senior at the University of Indianapolis. She is majoring in art education and plans to remain in Indianapolis, teaching elementary or middle school level art after graduating

Audrey Kline is a senior at the University of Indianapolis studying pre-art therapy with a studio art concentration in painting. She is new to photography in the last year but enjoys experimenting with how to craft creative representations through people and objects in the real world. Compared to fine arts, such as drawing or painting, photography activates her creativity in a completely new way.

Brandon Hickey is a student at the University of Indianapolis. He is studying psychology and creative writing. He has ambitions of one day becoming a professional writer. He is openly asexual and enjoys bringing light to the community.

Brooklyn Harpold is a sophomore music therapy major with a concentration in honors and music composition. She is currently the student music director for the University Chapel and the choir director for St. Andrew United Methodist Church. "Let Me Cry" is her first spoken-word piece and the first piece in a series entitled "Voices of Women," which highlights the struggles women face on an everyday basis.

Cambel Castle is a freshman at University of Indianapolis majoring in pre-art therapy. She enjoys creating art and writing poems. Her best works usually happen at night. She loves for her work to have deeper meanings or represent an experience or feeling. She hopes for the viewer/reader to feel some sort of emotion or connection when they look/read the work.

CariAnn Freed is a graduate student in the Department of Sociology at the University of Indianapolis and is especially interested in how education and community come together to push people to new heights. It is her dream to see every person see their world in new ways and to reach their greatest potential through identity development, community bonds, and leading first with our passions to find our purpose. Poetry is just one facet of all of her many passions and has been an active channel in discovering her purpose.

Cassi Dillon is a senior professional writing major.

Catherine Platter is a senior at UIndy studying pre-art therapy with a studio art major and a concentration in drawing. She enjoys using her art to create the idea of escapism and the alteration of our daily lives.

Chloe Crockett is a senior pursuing a music therapy degree with a concentration in composition at the University of Indianapolis. She is an accomplished pianist, composer, and studio teacher. She has won awards in both piano and music composition statewide. She has also published multiple of her works and been featured as a performer for an international conference.

Christopher Schmidt majored in English at DePauw University many years ago, where he focused on poetry writing. Today, he is a biological anthropologist who has had the great fortune of publishing many articles and book chapters in his areas of expertise. He, however, has never stopped writing poetry, and he maintains a sincere interest in creative writing that allows him to wrestle with relentlessly persistent concerns, concepts, and feelings.

Coda Barger is a freshman at UIndy and majors in human biology. While working within the forensic field is their passion, they also strive to be a published poet.

Danielle Shaw is a senior at UIndy studying English and secondary education. She takes great pride in her eccentric Twitter locations and writing poetry meant to be read in a gas station bathroom.

Dean Wiseman has been a professor in the Department of Biology for ten years here at UIndy. Before joining the faculty, he previously was a faculty member at Indiana University School of Medicine, the Medical College of Georgia, and the University of Montana, but all of his undergraduate and graduate education occurred here in Indiana and his home town of Indianapolis. He became interested in photography primarily through his mom, who has been an avid amateur photographer most of her life. His favorite subjects involve architecture, design, and travel photography, but he is also hoping to do more astrophotography and caving-oriented photography in the future.

Destini Mink is a psychology and English (creative writing) double major and is set to graduate in 2023. She has always enjoyed writing and has never shared her poetry before, but she thought *Etchings* would be the perfect place to do that.

Emma Knaack is a sophomore professional writing and creative writing major with an honors concentration at the University of Indianapolis. She is *Etchings* magazine's managing editor for issue 34.1, editorial assistant for Indy *Her Campus*, and a member of Phi Alpha Epsilon. In her free time, she enjoys thrifting, reading manga, watching anime, and listening to Korean and Japanese music.

Emma Warner is a senior pre-art therapy major with a sociology minor. She loves making functional ceramic pieces and gifting water-color cards to her loved ones. Warner hails from North Texas and moved to Indy for school. She is one of the co-Chairs for UIndy's PRIDE group and loves connecting to others and educating through this group.

Grace Carrender is a freshman studying secondary education and English with the hope of being a middle or high school English teacher. In her free time, she enjoys reading mystery novels, running a mental health advocacy account, listening to Declan McKenna, and antique shopping with her mom.

Hannah Jones is a senior visual communication design major and marketing minor at the University of Indianapolis. While at UIndy, she has been an ambassador for UIndy Admissions and a graphic designer for the Professional Edge Center. She has also served as the social media coordinator for two service organizations, Circle K and Glamour Gals. Hannah recently completed a summer graphic design internship with Anthem.

Heather Dawson is in her junior year at the University of Indianapolis, and she is following her dream to become a music therapist. She is a skilled vocalist, pianist, composer, and performer. She has performed and recorded with many different renowned musicians. She currently sings professionally with a local band, The Roundups, who have recently recorded an album of original material.

Hope Coleman graduated from the University of Indianapolis in 2021 with a degree in English, creative writing. She is an author and illustrator currently working on a full-length poetry collection and spends her free time exploring the United States, and, specifically, the midwest, for creative inspiration.

Jes Brockman Artemiev is studying visual communication design and photography at the University of Indianapolis. She has an Associate degree in fine art and probably something like a Master's degree in electives. She lives in Indianapolis with her husband, Ivan, and two cats, Behemoth (Biggie) and (Special Agent Dale) Cooper.

Julia Swindeman is an undergraduate student at the University of Indianapolis. While she does not study creative writing, she has always enjoyed writing and poetry. She takes every opportunity to write about feelings and emotions that she cannot decipher. She often does not know how she feels until she writes it down.

Karen L. Newman is an Associate Professor in the English Department at the University of Indianapolis, where she offers courses in teaching English as a second language (TESOL), composition, literature, modern arts, and service-learning. Her research interests include teacher professional development and international education. An avid world traveler, she has lived abroad for more than twenty years and visited thirty-five countries. She serves on the Board of Women Writing for (a) Change—Bloomington and enjoys the healing powers of the arts, especially writing creative nonfiction and experimenting with ceramics and photography.

Karina Camacho is a criminal justice major and graduated from Crawfordsville High School.

Kim Owen is a senior majoring in creative writing and minoring in professional writing at UIndy. She is excited for what her future holds after this year. She discovered her passion for writing especially as she prepared for her capstone project, a novel titled "A Shield Maiden's Challenge." She has had poems published in the past with *Etchings*, so she chose to contribute to Etchings as a staff member. Through her UIndy journey, she's been involved with KWS a couple of semesters, a Sigma Tau Delta member, this semester's Etchings' Whirling Prize team, and an English mentor for freshman English majors. Her other joys in life are her miniature schnauzer, Izzy, and her family who have been extremely supportive.

Kristen Taylor is a senior at the University of Indianapolis majoring in art therapy and has a minor in psychology.

Mackenzie Hyatt is a senior at UIndy and is majoring in four-field anthropology. Her favorite book is *A Thousand Splendid Suns* by Khaled Hosseini, and she wishes she could sit still long enough to read War & Peace. She would like to remind you that you are loved.

Maiya Johnson is a graduate of the University of Indianapolis with a Bachelor of Arts in professional writing. She is twenty-three years old and lives in a Walmart bakery constantly writing and volunteering. She enjoys workshopping her peer's writing, writing, mental breakdowns, conspiracy theories, and her morning coffee. Her biggest goal is to "be happy."

Mary Redman is a retired high school English teacher who currently works part time supervising student teachers for University of Indianapolis and volunteers as a docent at the Indianapolis Museum of Art at Newfields. She has had poems published in *Bangor Flying Island, Northwest Indiana Literary Review, Snapdragon: a Journal of Healing, Tipton Poetry Journal, So It Goes*, and elsewhere. One of her poems received a Pushcart nomination in 2019.
Mia Lehmkuhl is a freshman at UIndy majoring in entrepreneurship and minoring in finance. She has loved writing since before

she can remember. Her aspirations after graduating are to earn her MBA and pursue owning her own business.

M.J. Loria is an assistant professor of cognitive psychology in the Department of Psychological Sciences. They are awake and present.

Nicholas Jackson just wants to make art that'll make someone's day.

Olivia Cameron is a sophomore at UIndy. She is majoring in English (creative writing & professional writing) and hopes to become a published author and English professor one day. In addition to being co-Design Editor for *Etchings* 34.1, she is currently the Opinion Editor for *The Reflector.* She would like to give a shout out to her husband Benjamin Cameron and her cats Joni and Ripley.

Olivia Williams is from the Midwest and currently lives in Lebanon, Indiana. Their poems, as well as a short story of theirs, have appeared in *Etchings* vol. 33.2, 33.1, & 33.2. Their short story "We had coffee. We smiled." was chosen by Indiana Poet Laureate Adrian Matejka as the Runner Up for the Dorlis Gott Armentrout Award in *Etchings* vol 33.2. Olivia's poem "Betrayal" also received an Honorable Mention Award from R. Flowers Rivera in the University of Indianapolis' English Department Awards.

Pamela Smith is a graphic designer and illustrator at UIndy. She is currently in her third year of her degree and looks forward to the future. She loves tabletop games and designing characters.

Riley Childers is an alumna of the University of Indianapolis who loves writing and photography. She enjoys exploring Indiana for possible photo opportunities and hopes to expand her adventures outside of her home state.

Robert Springer wanted to exercise his rusty poetic skills by writing a sonnet and decided to write an updated version of the well-known and loved poem by Spencer, "One Day I Wrote Her Name

Upon the Strand." How well he did that is up to you.

Sabrina Camargo graduated from UIndy with a BS in psychology and criminal justice in May '21 and a MA in sociology in May '22. She is also a staff member in the Office of Admissions sharing her love for UIndy with prospective students.

Sam Jackson is a professional writing major who enjoys creative writing in his free time. Specifically, poetry is his favorite, and he hopes to publish his work someday in the future.

Savannah Harris is a left-handed senior at the University of Indianapolis with a major in creative writing and minors in professional writing and literary studies. She has an interest in writing fiction, poetry, and flash stories, which have been published in the *Penultimate Peanut Magazine, Etchings*, and *Neutral Spaces Magazine,* and she was the recipient of the 2020 Lucy Monro Brooker Poetry Award and 2021 Roberta Lee Fiction Award. Her plans are to graduate from UIndy and enroll in an MFA program, bringing her two cats along for whatever journey awaits.

Sierra Durbin is a sophomore at the University of Indianapolis and is majoring in creative writing and minoring in music. She performs in three choirs at the school, including the new Greyhound Sound Show Choir. Sierra is a writer at Her Campus and participates in UIndy Film Club. Besides singing and writing being her major passions in life, she also loves fashion, dance, and photography. Her work has been published in her high school's literary magazine as well as *Etchings*. She is working on becoming an influencer and internet performer under the name "Sierrallstar" and publishing more literature.

Sydney Nichols is currently a freshman at UIndy majoring in pre-art therapy. She finds inspiration for artwork in other people: conveying their experiences and emotions. A big reason for her interest in art therapy is to help others realize and work through their own emotions through art.

Sydney Smith is a freshman at the University of Indianapolis studying communications with an emphasis in electronic media. Sydney loves to travel and take photos, and she hopes to help people to see the beauty of simplicity through her work.

Sydnie Foster is a senior at the University of Indianapolis majoring in social work. She enjoys being active, helping people, and playing softball.

Trey Nobbe is a sophomore at the University of Indianapolis. He is studying data analytics and is a member of the Strain Honors' College. He enjoys writing as a creative outlet as it lets him create new worlds or ideas as well as express some of the hardships of his life.

Zeke Fredrickson is a senior at the University of Indianapolis studying visual communication design.

Zoe Wilkinson is a creative writing major and professional writing minor at the University of Indianapolis. They strive to write about mental health, disability, and LGBTQIA+ issues through both personal stories and original characters. They are a proud nonbinary and sapphic queer and enjoy creating character-based digital artwork in their free time.

Resources

If you are struggling, there are resources available:

UIndy Counseling Center
Health Pavilion, Suite 109
Hours: Monday-Friday, 8a.m. - 12p.m. and 1p.m. - 4p.m.
uindy.edu/studentcounseling/

From the *UIndy Counseling Center* website:
"[Dial 211] is a resource database that can help you find local health, human, and social service organizations. These may include locations that provide food or clothing, shelter, affordable housing, childcare, employment opportunities, utility assistance, and mental health services."

Be Well Indiana
www.bewellindiana.com

Call for Submissions

Etchings Magazine Volume 34 Issue 2, Spring 2022
Submissions due at 11:55 pm EST on January 31, 2022

Guidelines for Submission

• All UIndy students, faculty, staff, and alumni are invited to submit.
• All accepted undergraduate prose and poetry submissions will be considered for the Dorlis Gott Armentrout Award.
• Up to three short stories or creative nonfiction essays, five poems, five visual materials, and five audio files may be submitted.
• Visual submissions: for best print results, consider the 5.5 x 8 portrait page with .25 margins and flatten files to 300 ppi *.tiff CMYK 8 bit files.
• Poetry and Prose: present poems as single-spaced and prose double-spaced with both formatted in Microsoft Word (.doc, .docx, or .odt) in a 12-point font.
• Audio: submit *.mp3 files, and present scores/lyrics following the guidelines for visual or poetry submissions above.
• *Etchings Magazine* has a blind submission process, so please do not include any personal identifiers in your submission files (this information will be provided through Submittable when you submit your work).

Learn more about Etchings Press at etchings.uindy.edu

Submit work at etchings.submittable.com

We do not accept email submissions. Please create a free account at submittable.com or sign in using Facebook.

For questions, email us at etchings@uindy.edu

Follow us @uindyetchings on the platforms below:

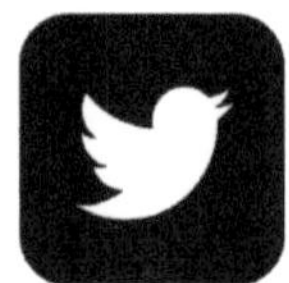

COLOPHON

Interior text is set in the Marion font family.
The cover font is in Didot.

www.ingramcontent.com/pod-product-compliance
Ingram Content Group UK Ltd.
Pitfield, Milton Keynes, MK11 3LW, UK
UKHW062309290726
14090UKWH00018B/963